THE
WELL-NOURISHED ARTIST

8 Ways to Feed Your Creative Soul

To Berandette~

Here's to publishing your beautiful book!

Christine Burke ♡

CHRISTINE BURKE

The Well-Nourished Artist
Copyright 2018 by Christine Burke

The content of this book is for general instruction only. Each person's physical, emotional, and spiritual condition is unique. The instruction in this book is not intended to replace or interrupt the reader's relationship with a physician or other professional. Please consult your doctor for matters pertaining to your specific health and diet.

Publisher:
Wholistic Healing, LLC

To contact the author, visit:
www.liveyourcreativity.com

ISBN-10: 0-692-11888-8
ISBN-13: 978-0-692-11888-7

Cover design: Amie Olson
Book design: Amie Olson

Printed in the United States of America

DEDICATION

*This book is dedicated to my mom - who fed my "Art Spirit"
healthy foods from the beginning,
and to the "Art Spirit" that resides in all of us!*

CONTENTS

FOREWORD

Live Your Creativity

The beauty of art itself is the creative spirit. In fact, it is the "Art Spirit." How hard is that to find? It begins with opening up to your passion and giving yourself permission. If that takes place, opportunities come in the most unorthodox ways. As Wayne Dyer (the motivational speaker) once said, "You collect allies along the way, people who see your passion and they want to help you succeed."

Robert Henri (from the Ashcan School of Art) wrote a book called *The Art Spirit*. I was fortunate to come across it at the beginning of my career. It changed my life. Indeed, you do come across brothers and sisters in the art field. One of those is Christine Burke. Her passion for life helped her create these next pages. Her love for art and the creative soul have shaped who she is today. People will find that her words in this are more than a book, but a way to look in oneself and discover more roads are possible in their lives; after all, sharing one's passion is contagious.

Enjoy!
Karl J. Kuerner
Artist

INTRODUCTION

Dream in Color

"When the artist is alive in any person, whatever his kind of work may be, he [or she] becomes an inventive, searching, daring, self-expressing, creature. He becomes interesting to other people. He disturbs, upsets, enlightens, and he opens ways for a better understanding. Where those who are not artists are trying to close the book, he opens it, shows there are still more pages possible."

The Art Spirit - Robert Henri

Is this Book for you?

Calling all artists — painters, actors, songwriters, poets, writers and sculptors who struggle with carving out time for their creative endeavors — this book is for you.

This book is for the future artists too! I believe we all have a creative spark inside, but some of us need help igniting it. This book will guide you so you can begin your creative journey. It will help you dig deeper and uncover your "Art Spirit." It will help you see the benefits of what adding creativity to your life can do for you and for everyone you encounter.

This book is for the starving artist who longs for something more, who desires to be well-nourished.

The Well-Nourished Artist integrates two topics that have been near and dear to me since the beginning of my life: Art and Health. My mom recalls that I started doodling as soon as I could hold a pencil, and that I started begging for salads and vegetables before I was two years of age. She was afraid I was too young to eat these foods and might choke. However, she gave in to my persistent begging.

Now, this isn't to say that these two things were always in my life.

Like many of us, I spent a lot of time denying and running from the artist within and dulling my senses with unhealthy habits. I went back and forth with healthy eating and spent years stifling my creative dreams.

Another topic that has been near and dear to me since the beginning is praying and a strong belief in a Higher Power that I like to call God. Creativity isn't possible without it and I do make mention of God, Angels and our Guides throughout the book; however, you may replace these words with what feels right for you.

How to Use this Book

"Well done is better than well said."

- Albert Einstein

This book will help you get started on the right actions to take immediately. It is broken down into eight ways to feed your creative soul, each way is a strategy to help you build on your creative journey. Incorporated throughout the book are my personal stories and clients' stories to demonstrate how these strategies can be used in everyday life. There are activities at the end of each chapter to help you integrate these strategies into your life.

The journey begins with gratitude because without gratitude in our lives we remain closed off to the wisdom of the universe and our God-given talents.

In this book, you will learn:

- That it is okay to release things that are bothering you and you will see how this can bring you into a state of appreciation.

- To let go of stories that are holding you back.

- How to use your uncomfortable emotions to create so you can move emotions out of your body. This is so beneficial for your health and well-being.

- To get in touch with your inner dialogue and observe it so it isn't controlling you and taking up your energy. You will understand that there are two conflicting voices inside: your intuitive voice and the shadow voice. There is also an observer of these voices. We will befriend the shadow voice, which will enable you to listen to the intuitive voice so you can take inspired action.

- How to incorporate self-care rituals into your daily routine. I discovered there are two types of self-care-pampering and grown-up self-care. I will explain the difference so that you can integrate both kinds of self-care into your life.

- How to say no to the things you don't want to do because when you say yes when you mean no, nobody around you benefits.

- About foods that give you sustained energy so you can replace those "go to" carbs with foods that will nourish you and help you go after your creative dream. This book will give you the opportunity to get creative in the kitchen and enjoy this time so that you can create fast and healthy meals so you are prepared ahead of time.

- How to be brave and bold while you create so you can take this concept and extend it into other areas of your life.

The journey ends with the opportunity for you to create your own masterpiece. I have included a painting lesson from one of my paint parties. It is for a painting called Bonfire. There are written directions as well as a link to a slideshow. Included in the directions is a list of materials so all you need to do is grab the materials and carve out some time for your creative soul.

Let's face it — it is hard to carve out time for ourselves and our creative dreams in this world that is continually trying to get us off track.

The Well-Nourished Artist will give you a roadmap to help you get focused and surrender so you can see that creativity isn't something that needs to be forced or put into a compartment — it is something that flows through us naturally when we learn to let go and listen.

Are you ready to stop that inner struggle and make space for this creative and healthy being?

Are you ready to have energy?

Are you ready to invite this creative being into every area of your life?

Let the creative adventure begin!

MY STORY

Metamorphosis

"There is no greater agony than bearing an untold story inside you."

- Maya Angelou

It was late on a cold winter night. I finished nursing my newborn son and swaddled him in a warm blanket and placed him in his bassinet near my bed. Then I headed to the laundry room and put my son's tiny clothes in the dryer. "How could one baby create so much laundry?" I asked myself.

I walked to the kitchen and picked up a toy that I had almost tripped on and tossed it in the toy box. I gulped down the rest of my white wine and then finished the dinner dishes. I went to the pantry and grabbed some potato chips and poured myself another glass of wine. Spotting my sketchbook on the table, I heard a gentle voice inside say, "Sketching will help you relax and feel good." But I silenced that voice with a handful of chips and a big swig of wine. I sat for a few minutes to try and relax. As I placed my empty wine glass in the sink, I heard a loud voice inside say, "You need to go on a diet; you are getting fat!"

On the way back to my bedroom, I checked in on my two-and-a-half-year-old toddler who was sleeping peacefully in her new big-girl bed. Exhausted, I kissed her on her cheek and headed back to my bedroom. Before I jumped into bed, I peeked in on my son. His eyes were fluttering, and a smile flashed across his face. It appeared as if he was dreaming a happy dream.

I thought of my happy dreams — I wanted to paint and write. Since I was a little girl, I had dreamed of writing and illustrating a children's book. My mom, an avid reader, took us to the library every week and I got lost in the world of books. I doodled the characters from the stories I read every chance I got.

I smiled as I stared at my sleeping baby and a voice inside convinced me that it wasn't the time to even be thinking of this pipe dream. After all, I was busy with my family, and there is no money in art. "Don't be selfish!" the voice shouted.

As I snuggled into my bed, I realized it felt like Groundhog Day. Wake up with a headache (because I drank wine to relax), feed the kids, do laundry, clean, load my kids in the double stroller to take a walk, go on play dates, cook dinner and repeat the next day.

I had left a busy job of teaching kids with emotional problems to stay home with my kids, and I was so grateful to have this opportunity. But on a day-to-day basis, I had to be honest with myself … I felt like something was missing.

One day while I was dusting my bookshelf, *The Artist's Way* by Julia Cameron, a book that I read and studied like it was my bible several years prior, caught my attention. I stared at the front cover and flashed back to when this book came into my life. I was in my second year of teaching special education when a friend gave me a copy of the book. I loved teaching but at that time I also longed to find my way back to art. I took art in high school and was all signed up to attend art school in Philadelphia, but a twist of fate led me down a different path. I attended college for teaching instead. Something stirred inside me as I held the book again. I felt an excitement and remembered back to how I did the morning pages and the artist date faithfully before I had my kids.

I blew the dust off the book and smiled as I opened it again. The first thing that caught my eye was a quote by Carl Jung, "Nothing has a stronger influence psychologically on their environment and especially on their children than the unlived life of a parent."

"Aha, I thought … I must start painting and writing so I don't live my life through my children." I got this deep feeling that living my life through others wasn't good for anyone. At that moment, I knew I needed to make time for myself so that everyone in my life would benefit.

But how?

I started by adding the morning pages and artist dates back into my life.

The morning pages are three longhand pages that are done as soon as you wake up. I set my alarm and woke up before my kids the next day to do my morning pages.

The artist date is making time for yourself once a week to do something fun — play, explore or do an activity you love. I carved out time for artist date even if it meant getting someone to watch my kids.

I felt alive again, and a feeling of pleasure stirred inside me. Within months the demands of my young family became greater and I found myself caving into these everyday tasks, abandoning my creative soul yet again.

Until one day, I was getting dressed for a "same old dull, boring day." I was in my closet, and it felt like something was closing in on me. I felt so trapped in my own life. That is when I heard this faint but powerful voice inside firmly state, "Paint or drink heavily."

That day I knew I had a choice to make.

I didn't waste another moment. I immediately called the local art center and signed up for a painting class. I decided to paint instead of drink heavily, and I am forever grateful for this decision.

However, that didn't mean it all magically changed there. For me, it took many years to get to a creative and healthy place and, like all of us, I had many tests along the way. It has been my observation that creative people can get distracted easily. We can get very creative when it comes to making excuses and finding things to do to keep us away from our artistic work. Quite often we busy ourselves with all kinds of activities we have no desire to do.

So I did add painting to my life. It took some time, but I eventually found a great art teacher and tried to keep creativity in my life on a daily basis. I felt this inner calling that it was time to focus on creativity and health even when life got busy, and that it was time to prioritize.

A Temporary Detour from My Creative Soul

There can be times in our lives when we abandon our creative souls due to events in our lives that seem to take over.

When my son was eight years old he got sick, and I felt overwhelmed. He started developing stomach virus-like symptoms, skin rashes and dark circles under his eyes. His dark circles were so noticeable that one day a kid in his class asked him why he had two black eyes.

I was exhausted and tried everything to figure out what was wrong with him. My life felt hectic, and naturally I was so concerned about my child that the first two things to go in my life were my creative time and my healthy lifestyle. I felt like I had no time to create and next thing you know, I found myself eating carbs to help with my energy level, only to feel even worse after indulging.

One day after leaving his bedroom and seeing him curled up in the fetal position (unable to go to school yet again because of his severe stomach pains) I knew I had to do something. I had taken him to the doctors a few times and each time they reported that he had a stomach virus, but to me it seemed like it was something more.

I walked down my steps, and a voice inside said clearly to me, "It is a food allergy." As I reflect back, I realize that maybe it was the same voice that gave me the choice to "paint or drink heavily."

I listened and headed right to my computer to investigate. A little while later, I concluded from my research that my son had a gluten allergy or intolerance. That day we went to the store and bought gluten-free foods; not the boxed ones — real food. It felt good. I went gluten-free with him. His symptoms cleared up within a few weeks. This new way of living cleared our minds, helped us focus and gave us energy. We went to the doctor again and found that my son was allergic to wheat and barley and I was allergic to barley. The recommendation was to be gluten-free, which we were already doing. Not long after, my son started having the same symptoms with dairy, and so we gave up dairy. Giving up dairy seemed even harder to do. Sometimes we would go to bed hungry because we didn't know what to eat or I didn't have enough time to prepare due to our busy schedule.

I truly was a starving artist. I had abandoned my creativity and felt so drained of energy and life force. I needed help, so I prayed.

One sunny Saturday morning my prayers were answered. My son and I went to a new lunch place and no sooner did we sit down than I heard this kind voice ask, "Is this seat taken?" I looked up and saw a lady pointing to an open seat at our table. I replied, "No, please sit down," but I looked around and wondered why she asked to sit with us when there were open tables everywhere.

We engaged in a conversation right away. The friendly lady explained to us how she was recently diagnosed with a gluten and dairy allergy, so we had stories to share. She told us that she saw a health coach that helped her with recipes, ideas, accountability, etc. She grabbed a piece of paper and pen from her purse and proceeded to write down her name and number for us. We ate and continued to chat; it was like we knew her. I am convinced this sweet little lady crossed our path for a reason; she was a divine messenger.

I called the health coach, who was an Institute for Integrative Nutrition® graduate, that Monday and made an appointment. She guided us and gave my son advice. On hearing many of her suggestions for foods he could eat, he would reply, "I know, my mom gave me that last night." Her gentle support and advice were invaluable and really helped me stay on track and it also helped me not to feel so overwhelmed by this new way of life.

One day we were sitting at a table in Whole Foods with the health coach. She was guiding my son and he replied, "I know, my mom told me that." The health coach looked at me and with a smile, asked, "Did you ever think of becoming a health coach?" Then she proceeded to tell me all about Institute for Integrative Nutrition®.

I was intrigued, but then my guard went up and shut the idea down by saying firmly, "I am too busy!"

But little clues kept coming to me about this health coaching program. "Would it be beneficial for me to register for the program?" I wondered.

On a whim one day, I did it. I signed up. In hindsight, I know this was not a whim but my intuition guiding me to listen to my desires.

LEARNING FROM CLIENTS

We Dance in a Circle

"We are all in this together."

- Unknown

Becoming a health coach was one of the best decisions I ever made and a real turning point for me. I was already working with clients to help them tap into their creativity, tune into their intuition and discover their creative dreams. The health coaching piece added some depth to the work I did with them. I helped my clients go deeper with their daily struggles and helped them identify how they were starving themselves of creativity because they were busy filling themselves with food, alcohol and other distractions. I helped my clients find a balance between the food they put on their plate and what they fed their creative soul. As I integrated all the strategies that worked in my life with health and creativity, I also used them with my clients and others who feel this struggle on a daily basis.

The strategies are here in this book. I saw that my struggles were universal struggles, and I believe the strategies in this book can help you stop the inner struggle and live your most creative life.

I have clients who struggle with distractions. Instead of working on what they want to be working on, their creative dream, they make excuses. They let their inner dialogue of why they aren't good enough or why they aren't deserving take up all their energy. Whether it be a painting or a book or a business, they find excuses and distract themselves with things like eating, cleaning out closets or going out to obligatory lunches and visits.

I also have clients who feel they get too lost in creativity and want to keep going and they ignore things they need to take care of — so these artists don't even want to start. After working with this type of client, I realized that creativity doesn't have to be a separate compartment in our lives. Although at first, we might need to carve out time in our life for creativity and say no to the things that are distracting us, we can eventually realize that creativity is something you can add or bring to every area of your life.

I also saw how my clients had beliefs that there was no money in art, and they felt like they were just wasting their time on a career that would never pay off. I looked back and saw how I had this inner struggle for years, thinking I should do something more important than just make art. I saw how these beliefs held me back and kept me from creating. This led me to contemplate the whole myth of the starving artist. Why are we so programmed to believe that an artist must struggle and that we need to be poor and starving in order to create?

THE STARVING ARTIST
IS IT JUST A MYTH?

Summer Flowers

"To eat is a necessity but to eat intelligently is an art."

- Francois de Rochefoucauld

The term "starving artist" was believed to have originated during the Romanticism period of the late Eighteenth and early Nineteenth Centuries, which was a period that resisted order and idealization. The art during this period celebrated the individual and intuition; it dealt with emotions, imagination and vision. But somehow these visionary ideas and mindsets were diminished and were replaced with the starving artist mindset/myth.

A French novelist and poet named Henry Murger wrote Scenes de la Vie de Boheme in 1851 (the inspiration for the opera La Boheme). This writing conceptualized Bohemia. He wrote about himself and his artist friends who were struggling to get their work recognized. It was in his depiction of the artist experience that the idea of the starving artist became glamorized.

While researching this topic I found so many places such as art galleries, restaurants and other places of business named after the starving artist. It appears that we have romanticized this term to this day. Yet, at the same time, we resist it.

A starving artist is someone who will forgo material things so he/she can concentrate on their artwork.

It doesn't say anything about being poor or struggling. It merely states that he or she is willing to give up material things to follow their creative dream. I wonder if this could be the part we romanticize?

Ahh, the freedom of not having to manage so many material things. It seems to be a trend these days. At this time in society, many of us desire to give up material things in order to be happy. With all the trends towards decluttering and minimalism, we are seeing that there are many benefits to owning less. Many of us are happier and healthier with less stuff weighing us down.

I believe we need to question the poor and struggling part.

Does this myth unconsciously hold us back from being creative?

Many believe that the starving artist is indeed a myth that we were programmed to believe. This programming that was handed down to us makes it taboo for any young person to want to pursue a career in the arts. Their well-intended parents steer them away because they don't want them to be poor or struggle. The social programming wants us to conform, and being creative isn't about conforming. There is this belief that art is a calling and not a viable career. The idea that an artist must starve to create is just a silly notion and stifles so many of us from living our lives fully and creatively.

In many professions, you hear of people focusing on their passions and giving up material things so they can focus on their dreams or spend more time with the people they love. This doesn't mean they struggle; rather, it means they are adjusting their life to fit their desires. At first, the adjustments may be challenging, but they adjust because they want to feel passionate and alive.

Whether you want to make art your career or add it to your life and career, it is worth questioning the social programming around the myth of the starving artist. When we open up to the idea that we can be successful with art and dispel the fears we have around it, we can enjoy the freedom of our choices.

The Well-Nourished Artist will help you take a look at the social programming and shift it so we can not only dispel the starving artist myth but also nourish the mind, body and soul of the artist. It will allow you to flourish and create an inner life that feeds your "Art Spirit" and keeps it alive.

I believe creativity is our birthright. So when we buy into the myth of the starving artist, we shut down a resource that can make our lives feel more alive. This book will help you seek internal approval and create internal goals instead of giving that power away to an external force. It will guide you to look inside where the real power lies!

How does the starving artist become the well-nourished artist? Keep reading, and you will find out! I created eight ways to help you feed your creative soul that will not only help you in your work but in all areas of your life.

#1

PRACTICE GRATITUDE WITH A TWIST

Spring Fling

"Gratitude opens the door to … the power, the wisdom,

the creativity of the universe."

- Deepak Chopra

I smiled at my family as we sat at the dinner table, ready to eat. However, first we would take some time to share our gratitude. I started this tradition with my kids when they were little. We would either share our gratitude list before we ate or before they went to bed, depending on our schedule. On this particular evening I was grateful for the food on the table — sweet potato fries, honey lime chicken, a colorful salad and a family to share it with. I was also grateful for my art class that kept my "Art Spirit" alive. I turned to my son to listen to his list. Instead of reciting his gratitude list, he looked at me boldly and said, "You know sometimes there are things that I am not grateful for. Can I share them with you?"

My initial response was to say to him, "No! This is gratitude time, and we are focusing on gratitude. No complaints." But I took a deep breath and put my control freak on the back burner for a moment and made space to listen to my son.

He blurted out his complaints in two minutes and then went on to his gratitude list.

Wow, I thought, leave it to a kid to not sweep their feelings under the rug. To be able to complain (or I like to call it release) and then move on. I had been practicing gratitude for years and never thought to look at it in this light until my son brought this to my attention. I only thought of staying positive.

I remembered back to when I first started practicing gratitude. After reading The Artist's Way, another pivotal book came into my life called Simple Abundance by Sarah Ban Breathnach. (Looking back, I see how the universe gives you the books you need at just the right time in your life, and there is a perfect order to our individualized curriculum here on earth.) Sarah Ban Breathnach suggests that you keep a gratitude journal. Every night before you go to bed you write down five things you are grateful for in your life.

I added the gratitude journal to my list of tools along with the morning pages and the artist date. Unlike the morning pages and artist date, this tool stayed with me through the years even when life got busy.

When the book *Simple Abundance* came into my life I was teaching kids with emotional and behavioral problems. I loved teaching these kids and they taught me great life lessons which I will always carry with me; but I must admit day in and day out this job drained me. So, practicing gratitude at this time in my life was perfect.

I bought a journal and kept it on my nightstand. Every night I listed things I was grateful for, my list included simple yet specific ideas like: I am grateful this day is over; I am grateful so and so didn't throw any desks across the room today; I am grateful I only heard ten curse words today instead of the usual hundred.

It only took a few minutes to do it every night.

I experienced the ways gratitude opens the door and brings you into the present moment where creativity takes place. It is an essential part of the journey.

My son's insight helped me see that it was okay to release complaints or things we weren't grateful for in our life. Although I sometimes complained and released in my morning pages over the years, I felt guilty when I did it. I kept things bottled up and often pretended everything was okay on the outside. I tried to remain positive at all times but had such an aha moment when my son blurted out his negative feelings and then quickly shifted to his positive ones. I realized that the fight to stay positive all the time was exhausting me; I too needed to release my complaints, my feeling of unhappiness and my frustrations.

After that evening at the dinner table, my kids and I created a new ritual — we were allowed to talk about things we were grateful for and things we weren't so grateful for in our lives. This practice deepens our relationships with others. It gives us an understanding of the whole person and what that person might be going through on a particular day. It gives each of us a safe place to express some of our negative emotions without feeling guilty about it.

And so "Gratitude with a Twist" was born.

Gratitude with a Twist

Gratitude with a Twist is about being grateful while simultaneously accepting all of our human characteristics and feelings.

It is the balance or, as I like to call it, the dance between two things — being grateful yet knowing there are times that we need to release an angry, sad or complaining emotion from our body.

It is not about smiley face denial, pretending or sweeping things under the rug. Instead, it is about understanding that we are human. As Debbie Ford, author of The Dark Side of the Light Chasers, explains in her Shadow Work — "We each hold within us a trace of every human characteristic that exists."

When we accept this humanness, we permit ourselves to feel all the emotions, even the negative ones like anger and sadness, that go along with being human. We don't need to stuff or repress the feelings, which only come out later in some way that might not be in anyone's best interest. Instead, we learn how to use all our emotions and our human strengths and weaknesses to our advantage.

In life things can annoy us, people can annoy us, and feeling guilty about this or pretending this isn't present doesn't work long term.

Releasing things that are bothering us in a healthy way and accepting the darkness of being human allows the light to come in. Also, when something bugs us about another person or thing, it can give us a clue as to what is going on inside of us.

Carl Jung once said, "Everything that irritates us about others can lead us to a deeper understanding of ourselves."

Practicing Gratitude with a Twist can change your artwork and how you look at things. Also, when you allow yourself to practice gratitude yet also have this place of release, your artwork can be this safe place to feel everything, even the negative emotions. It is a place to release these emotions, thus making it more appealing to all who view it because it carries with it human emotions.

If I am feeling sadness or anger, I don't try deny it anymore. Instead I accept these emotions and express them through art. There will be more on this topic with Creative Way #3 — Create Motion with Emotions.

Activities

For now, we are going to practice some activities that will help you add gratitude to your life and also help you accept all of your human characteristics and feelings. Implementing these activities into your life is the first step in helping you reclaim and restore your "Art Spirit."

1. Take an Inventory of Your Strengths and Weaknesses

Get a piece of paper and fold it in half. Write your strengths on one side and your weaknesses on the other. I am touching on this now but this is a theme that runs throughout the book, and this activity lays the groundwork. This is not about judging yourself; however, it is about understanding that you are a human comprised of lights and darks. Discovering what your strengths and weaknesses are in this activity will help you use them both to your advantage.

I do this activity every so often, especially when I am having a hard time balancing my human qualities with my spiritual being. I find this is so freeing and gives you a better understanding of yourself. Writing down your strengths and weaknesses shifts something inside, and it helps you let go of the defenses you've built from trying to protect your weaknesses or prove your strengths.

If you are having a hard time with writing down either your strengths or weaknesses, elicit the help of a friend or family member. I remember doing this activity years ago and asking my young children if they could share with me one of my weaknesses. Their honesty was invaluable. I asked them each separately, and they basically both said the same thing. "Mom, when you decide you want to do something or something has to be done, you think everyone should drop what they are doing and listen." My daughter explained that it might be her time to watch a show, and if I want something done, all of a sudden I would go in and turn the TV off even though it is her planned TV time. I had just told her five minutes prior to shutting it off that she could watch a show.

What an "aha moment" for me when I realized that I did do that and I didn't need to defend it anymore. I realized that I am a person with a lot of energy who takes action all the time (sometimes to a fault), but I can learn to dial that down a little and I don't have to be so impatient and bossy. I can wait until the show is over and give everyone, including myself, a little bit of breathing room. Besides, I didn't like when people did this to me. I was so grateful for their honesty.

Deep down I'd always known this about myself; it felt so freeing to get it out into the open and not have to defend or deny it anymore. All at once, I realized the pros and cons of having a lot of energy. I always put so much pressure on myself and others around me to get things done. Sure, it can be a strength too, if I become aware of it and use it to my advantage.

Sometimes our strengths, or what we think are our strengths, can be more damaging than our weaknesses. For example, I once had a client who convinced herself that a strength of hers was that she was easygoing. She held on and defended it like it was the best strength anyone could have. We delved into this further and found that this strength was also a weakness. Since she convinced herself she was easygoing, she realized that this kept her from making boundaries. She said yes to everyone and everything and this created inner turmoil.

Another example is from a client who stated that her weakness was that she felt like she was rude and abrupt and spoke up too quickly to people when they asked something of her. She felt like she was being pulled in so many directions. We agreed that she was probably just trying to make boundaries, which is a strength. However, she felt bad about the way she handled these situations. We talked about how she could do this in a more grounded way; she could take a deep breath before she spoke or when someone asked something of her she could say, "Let me think about that." This way she gave herself some space to think about things and respond appropriately. This way she wouldn't make anyone, including herself, feel bad about the situation.

Taking an inventory like this will help you see that you don't need to hold on to or judge your strengths and weaknesses. Instead, you can accept them and use them to your best advantage. It prepares you for the "Gratitude with a Twist" work.

2. Start a Gratitude Journal

Buy a simple journal and keep it by your bedside. Either at night or in the morning, write a list of things you are grateful for. The list can be simple yet you can give specific examples like — I am grateful for the weather because I was able to take a longer walk. If you don't like to write, you can draw quick sketches of what you are grateful for each day. Here is your chance to welcome your "Art Spirit." You can use different colored markers to make your list or design your list in creative ways.

Remember, this is gratitude with a twist so you can also write things down that are bothering you. In this way you become aware of what you would like to change or shift in your life.

Some people choose to use two separate journals for this activity. Another option is to write what is bothering you on a piece of paper and then throw it out or burn it. This ritual act further helps us with the release.

3. Team Up with a Gratitude and Release Buddy

Practice Gratitude with a Twist with this buddy. You can quickly text each other in the morning or at night what you are grateful for, or you can call each other and share your lists or share them in person.

Give each other space and time to release; otherwise, these emotions stay trapped inside and can cause us trouble down the line. Let these things be heard in a safe place. These feelings are valid, and they are often key to realizing our desires. They can also show us what we want to bring into our lives. Keeping these emotions inside isn't healthy for anyone.

It is essential to recognize how holding in or denying emotions can affect our health. Releasing will improve your health and your creative work. What we do with these emotions (we will get into this in more detail with Creative Way #3) is pivotal to our health and well-being.

Now, this isn't to say that we let people go on and on about the same person, issue or subject. This isn't good for anyone either. Sometimes we need to hold up the stop sign. Friends don't let friends over-complain. Releasing has a different energy about it. When you get into a regular practice of this releasing, you will quickly be able to identify and feel the difference. Put a time limit on the release; two to five minutes at the most. The goal is to release and shift your mood, to take a look at what is bothering you and use your insights to help understand yourself and work through a situation.

Notice what words you are using over and over when releasing. One time my friend was using the word lazy over and over when talking about a coworker. I gently asked her, "Is there an area in your life where you are feeling lazy?"

A tear came to her eye, and she said, "Yes, I beat myself up inside and call myself lazy all the time because I never do the things I say I am going to do. I write a list of things I want to do for myself and never follow it."

This awareness gave her a deeper understanding of what was going on inside of her and allowed her to release and own what parts of herself she needed to own. This awareness created space for things to shift in her life.

I have taught this technique to my children and also use this technique with my clients. I have found time and time again that integrating the mix of gratitude and release in our lives gives us permission to live more fully.

4. A Gratitude Symbol

Have a symbol you carry with you to remind you of gratitude. It can be a piece of jewelry like a ring or a necklace. It can also be a word or a sign you hang in your home or workplace, someplace where you will see it frequently and it will serve as a daily reminder.

I have a pink quartz crystal that I carry with me in my purse to help me focus on gratitude. Whenever I am struggling all I need to do is reach in and touch this precious stone and I feel a shift.

You can also get creative with your symbol and choose or make something which reminds you of gratitude.

5. Write Gratitude Notes

Keep a running list of people to whom you can send a gratitude or thank you note. You can also dig into your past and think of people you might want to thank. Make a habit out of sending handwritten notes, texts or messages to people you appreciate. You can get creative with the notes and use markers, stickers or your artwork on cards. You can send gratitude notes to family, friends, acquaintances and business partners. Make this a daily or weekly practice. As you are writing the note, take a moment to contemplate what this person did for you and why you are grateful. Thank you notes benefit both the giver and the receiver. Reflecting on why you feel grateful is a magical step in reminding yourself that there is good in the world and you have a lot to be thankful for in life.

*"If the only prayer you ever say in your entire life
is thank you, it will be enough."*

- Meister Eckhart

6. Implement the Morning Pages Into Your Routine

Since the morning pages have had such an impact on my life and helped me uncover my "Art Spirit," I suggest you give this valuable tool from *The Artist's Way* by Julia Cameron a try in your life.

A helpful tip to make sure you do the morning pages is to have things ready to go the night before. Create the space. Place your journal out in a place where you like to write, then place a candle or a salt lamp and some crystals in this space. Set your coffee pot up the night before or get your teabag or warm drink prepared to go. Set the stage. Wake up fifteen minutes early and write! Also, it is suggested that you do it every day, but do not beat yourself up if you miss a day. Remember - you are human and we all have things going on and can sometimes get distracted.

Again, the morning pages are three longhand pages that are done as soon as you wake up. In the introduction I talked about how the morning pages came in and out of my life depending on what was going on. When this ritual finally stayed in my life consistently, I always started my day on a good note. (And yes, I am human and I also missed the occasional day. And still do!) Over the years I have filled hundreds of journals. These pages have become my therapy, my muse, my inspiration and a place to dump my thoughts and feelings.

Writing every day helped me question the social programming that society feeds to us — the set of rules we learned at an early age to help us conform and fit into society. Our family, church organizations, schools, teachers and peer groups all contribute to the process of socialization. As I poured my heart out in my journals, I realized that this programming left no room for the individual, because we were constantly searching for outside approval in our lives. Our goals and dreams seem to be rooted in what society wants for us. The morning pages helped me learn how to seek internal approval and create internal goals. It helped me break free of the social programming that was engrained inside of me and our society. It helped me question the myth of the starving artist and move towards creating a rich and fulfilling life.

While writing the morning pages, I discovered two different voices inside of me: the intuitive voice and the shadow voice. The shadow voice is always looking for drama and problems. I've also noticed that there is an observer inside watching these voices play a kind of mental tennis; back and forth they go and we often get confused about which voice we should listen to.

Understanding the concept that there are two conflicting voices and an observer of these voices can lead us to a better understanding of how to listen to that still, confident voice inside that is our intuition, also known as our art spirit. There will be more on this topic when you learn about Creative Way #4 – How to Surrender and Take Inspired Action. In the meantime, give the morning pages a try and see what you discover.

Here's to adding gratitude to your life and also accepting your humanness and knowing you might sometimes have things you are not grateful for that need to be honored, listened to and released. Practicing Gratitude with a Twist leads us into a deeper appreciation for all things and puts us in a higher vibration of love, which helps us live more authentically. When we feel grateful, yet make space for our emotions to be released, our hearts are lighter, and it feels like a weight is lifted from us. It is God's way of saying, "Now go and love and do what you came here to do."

"Gratitude makes sense of our past,
brings peace for today,
and creates a vision for tomorrow."

- Melody Beattie

#2

IDENTIFY YOUR CREATIVITY THIEVES

Soul Dreams

"If people aren't laughing at your dreams,

your dreams aren't big enough."

- Robin Sharma

I walked into my house, slammed the front door and threw my painting face-down on my dining room table. I didn't realize my three-year-old daughter was in the next room. She came running to greet me.

"Mommy, Mommy what did you paint today?"

I wanted to throw my painting in the trash. My daughter jumped up on the dining room chair, turned the painting over and said, "Oh Mommy what a pretty painting. Is that me and my brother in the picture?" I smiled at her but the voice of my art teacher kept ringing in my ear.

"You have absolutely no talent." It was like a broken record.

Since I was a child, I dreamed of writing and illustrating a children's book. I was so glad I decided to sign up for an art class because it was either that or drink heavily.

Excited about finally following this dream, I showed up to the first class with all my new supplies. The dream slowly turned into a nightmare when the teacher criticized every move I made. I told him of my idea of writing and illustrating a children's book, and he laughed at me and told me I had absolutely no talent. He went on to say that the ideas I had in my head were just too hard for someone like me. According to him, I was the worst student in the class.

After a few months of this abuse, I longed to quit. I remember a friend saying, "You can't quit; quitters never win." This is one of society's programmed beliefs, and I knew I needed to protect my dream and so I didn't listen to my friend's advice — I quit. Or, as another friend pointed out to me later on, "You didn't quit; you fired him."

My shadow voice and intuitive voice really went back and forth. A battle inside began. My shadow voice argued that the teacher was right, and I was crazy to think I could achieve this pipe dream. My intuitive voice gently urged me to keep going. I decided to do a little soul-searching. I realized that this pattern of teachers criticizing me started back in grade school. As a child there probably wasn't much I could have done about this situation, but as an adult, I knew I was ready to take action. I wanted to clear and rewrite these stories of criticism so I could embark on my creative journey.

Determined, I started to think of ways to uncover my inner artist and not be controlled by words that other people said to me. Instead, I tried to use their words of criticism to help me move forward.

I continued my morning pages and I painted on my own after I left the class. These tools helped me find my way into my own heart and also helped me listen to my intuition. I started writing about all my personal stories that were holding me captive. The morning pages and painting helped me get the buried stories up and out of me. Some days I felt like it would have just been easier to listen and believe the cruel words of the art teacher. But there was something inside of me that wouldn't let me give up on my creative dream.

Recently, I heard Brené Brown say in a video about her new book *Braving the Wilderness,* "Our worth and belonging are not negotiated with other people. We carry those things inside our hearts." As I reflected back to that time in my life, I realized that this was what had shifted for me: I was no longer willing to negotiate myself when it came to creativity. There was this fire inside me that wasn't going to allow me to give up on my dream. I was no longer willing to give my power away to someone else's opinion. Someone laughing in my face wasn't going to stop me. Maybe, just maybe, this "mean art teacher" story gave me fuel and deep inner strength to stand up for my creativity, which has helped me also guide others to stand up for their creativity. Maybe it's been a blessing in disguise. I now see this situation as a gift.

As I was writing this chapter for the book, my home team, the Philadelphia Eagles, won the Super Bowl as the underdogs. This inspiring team, despite all odds and everyone against them, came from behind and won with prayers, faith, surrender and belief in God. It might sound crazy and a little far-fetched to compare my inner win of not giving up on my creative dream to a Super Bowl win, but this is what it felt like to me.

The Underdog

What if we took these opinions of others and used them to help us shift things? We can use the opinions and the harsh words to our advantage instead of using them to make us a victim.

Jason Kelce, the center for the Philadelphia Eagles, gave the most amazing speech at the Super Bowl parade on the topic of being an underdog. Dressed in a mummer's costume, he passionately spoke about the team's underdog status and exploded with a list of players on the team (and the coach), explaining how they were underdogs and how the media criticized each one of them. Then he went and stated boldly — "The underdog is a hungry dog and hungry dogs run faster." The crowd cheered. Everyone seems to love an underdog. I believe that the underdog also takes more risks because they feel like they have nothing to lose.

What risk can you take today?

Can you think of an underdog story that happened to you?

Are you ready to shift your stories and use them to your advantage?

When you make up your mind about something and feel it in your heart, there are specific actions you have to take, but it can happen. Naysayers are always going to show up; they don't mean what they say. They are merely projecting their fears and beliefs. Use what they say as rocket fuel, use what they say as stepping stones, and place these stepping stones on your path and, like Henry David Thoreau said, "Go confidently in the direction of your dreams."

As I was soul-searching after the "mean art teacher" incident, another story that I carried with me for so long popped into my mind, a story from first grade that needed to be released and rewritten.

I remembered sitting at my desk in first grade with an array of colorful crayons spread out on my desk. I was so lost in my drawing I was creating and so happy. We were doing the popular activity of drawing what we wanted to be when we grew up. I wanted to be a singer so I created this elaborate stage with fancy curtains and me standing on the stage with a beautiful pink gown and long flowing hair. I was so proud of the drawing I created. The teacher announced time was almost up, so I quickly drew a bunch of circles below the stage, it was the audience. It came time to hand it in, and a boy in my class laughed at my circles and said, "You don't know how to draw people."

Do you know what I told myself for years?

You guessed it. "I can't draw people."

Never mind the great drawing of the person I drew on stage; that somehow didn't count.

This voice still shows up to this day when I go to draw people. I just listen to it and laugh, knowing I don't need to take it seriously.

Shortly after doing this inner work, I found an art teacher who didn't criticize anybody's work. He taught everyone to paint what they love. This was a lesson he learned from his mentor, Andrew Wyeth.

His name is Karl Kuerner.

Finding Karl makes me think of the quote, "When the student is ready, the teacher will appear." Rather than pushing and trying to make things happen to find a new teacher, I listened to my intuitive voice, took inspired action and, before you know it, a teacher landed on my path who helped me rewrite all my previous stories through the way he taught.

Creativity Thieves Defined

In working with others, I have found that many of us have these two or three people who gave us their unsolicited opinion about our creativity and this opinion can still be holding our creativity back today.

I call them our "Creativity Thieves."

Most likely they didn't intend to steal our creativity. These people were stating their opinion and/or projecting a fear or a belief they had onto us. Who says their opinion was right or true? Yet we took it as truth and started believing what they told us rather than listening to what we felt about what we created. We shut ourselves down to listen to someone else.

What if we changed these stories and let them go?

Changing our stories is easier said than done, but I will guide you through a meditation at the end of this chapter that will help you.

Art and creativity are an expression of who we are, an extension of us, a way to get to know ourselves better. How can that be categorized into right or wrong? It really can't be.

These opinions from the "Creativity Thieves" in our lives shut down way more than just painting on canvas.

Although picking up that brush can be a bold start, our "Creativity Thieves" stories make us second guess and question ourselves when it comes to creativity. Something that once came naturally to us is now filled with feelings of nervousness and fear. These stories robbed us of the creative life force that is within all of us.

As Colette Baron-Reid states, "Your life is the most creative thing you can do. Don't ever say you're not creative. Every action, every choice, every thought creates reality."

We can think of everything we do as a creation — the way we raise our kids, the way we dress, the way we show up in our work, the way we love, the way we create meals, eat and move our bodies.

Creativity is a life force we all can tap into. Sometimes, in order to tap into this life force we need to share and let go of the stories that are holding us back. Then we can live a creative life. I find it fascinating that some people will come right into a painting workshop I am teaching and tell me their childhood stories of creativity.

Just recently I was hosting a paint night for a group of therapists; they were having a workshop day for their practice, which included information sessions, team bonding and relaxation. I wasn't there five minutes when one of the therapists came up to me and shared a story that happened to her in kindergarten, a story that she believed deflated her creativity. She explained that when she was in kindergarten the teacher gave them a drawing assignment, she didn't remember the details of the assignment. The teacher gave them about twenty minutes to work on it. She remembered using crayons and working on it the whole time, even though most of the kids were finished early. When the teacher came around to look at the drawings, she said to her, "It took you all this time to do THAT?"

She explained that it embarrassed her and made her never want to draw again. From that point on she thought she was a terrible artist. Throughout the paint party, we talked about how she could rewrite this story. She said that it felt weird for her when she was painting; she kept looking at other people's paintings and comparing herself. It brought back the same feeling that her work wasn't right or good enough. We can let these feelings come up again without judgement so we can release them.

She told me later that when she went home and showed her husband, he thought it was terrific, and she stated she would love to do another painting class.

Other people have stories so deeply buried that all they can do is actively voice that they are just not creative. They are unconsciously repeating these stories like a broken record, so much so that they believe they are true. What we need to realize is these stories can be dug up and released. We can rewrite these stories.

For some, it is apparent which stories are holding them back. Others may need to do some digging. When people come into my workshops and stand with their arms crossed, insisting that they are not creative, I know it is time to roll up my sleeves and help them go deeper.

I have this one friend who came to some of my workshops, and she was so insistent that she just wasn't creative. I kept assuring her that it is our birthright to be creative and this story that she wasn't creative must have started somewhere in her childhood. She remained convinced of her lack of creativity until she came to one of my meditation/visualization workshops. We were in the middle of the mediation when, out of nowhere, she yelled out, "My second-grade teacher told me I drew rain all wrong." Bam! We finally found one of her creativity thieves.

After the meditation, we discussed her findings. I said to her, "How can you draw rain wrong?" We laughed and agreed. She then said, "It felt great to share this story out loud. I felt validated." She then repeated, "Yeah, how can you draw rain wrong? It was my interpretation of what rain looked like." She realized how this story deflated her and made her feel stupid. After this incident that happened to her in second grade, she didn't want to share her art with anyone. We then took time to draw images we received in the meditation. She drew a dancer in a long, red, swaying dress. It was bold and she proudly shared her art with everyone in the group.

I have another client that took years to get to her creativity thieves. She too was stuck on the story that she just wasn't creative. With some gentle persuasion to explore and share, she finally realized it was her older sisters who would always take over and do her creative projects for her. They had good intentions and wanted to help her. However, she believed she never really created anything on her own, and so she made up the story that she wasn't creative and never would be.

Other clients have released stories where they were told how amazing something they created was so, as a result, they decided to shut down. They were afraid they wouldn't be able to create something that good again.

Activities

Whatever type of story you might have told yourself, I am going to take you on a journey where you get to identify the story, release it and then rewrite it using the meditation below. The meditation is followed by other activities.

1. Meditation

The meditation is a broken into five steps. First, I will have you get comfortable and then I will lead you through a series of questions to help you describe your creative place. Once you find this creative place, you are going to ask for stories that might have taken your creativity away from you. They might not come to you right away, but just taking time to do this meditation helps you make space to uncover them. The stories might come to you after the meditation when you are not thinking about them, or you can do the meditation again. Then we will create a painting or drawing of this place. Finally, we will rewrite these stories. I suggest that you do the first three steps in one sitting and then come back to the last two steps at a later time.

I got the idea for this meditation from my dreams. After I started taking classes with Karl, I kept having recurring dreams of this most beautiful place; it was a cross between somewhere that looked like Greece and Italy. I am not sure if it is even a real place, but to me it is. In my dream I saw stone benches, fountains and beautiful gardens everywhere. It was surrounded by an ocean. After dreaming of this place, I felt such peace the next day.

One night many years ago, I was working on a painting and was getting frustrated. I was trying to paint a glass vase — this was before Google, so I was on my own. But not really, because that night in my dreams, I dreamt of my beautiful creative place, and Karl showed up and taught me how to paint the glass vase. I woke up the next morning with the information, finished the painting, and sold it shortly after that. I decided that this was my creative place, a visualization I could use anytime I needed to tap into my inner artist.

Let this mediation be your guide to help you dig deeper. I have found it to be helpful that when we can picture this creative place as a visual inside it is easier to go there, time and time again when we want to connect to that creative place inside.

Step 4 - Create a Painting or Drawing and Rewrite Your Story/Stories

After the meditation, do a little thumbnail of your creative place. Thumbnail sketches are small drawings done very quickly with no corrections. An artist usually does several thumbnail sketches of the same idea. Use the ideas from your thumbnail sketch and create a painting or a drawing of your creative place. Place this creation in a special place, like an altar to remind you of your inner artist.

Step 5 - Rewrite Your "Creativity Thieves" Story/Stories

The stories don't need to be elaborate, just a quick story to help you reprogram. Here is my story that I rewrote from first grade -

Rewind 45 Years …

I have more time for the activity and draw people in the audience. Then when we are handing in the assignment, the little boy says to me, "Wow, look at your people. They are so good!"

2. Write a List of Creative Things You Have Done in Your Life

This is so helpful in keeping your art spirit alive. Make sure you add to this list daily or weekly.

3. Do Something for Your Art Spirit Every Day

As I mentioned earlier, sometimes we don't even want to start creating because we feel like we can get so lost in the process and forget about our everyday tasks. This activity will help you see that we don't need to put creativity in a separate compartment. It is the beauty of the "Art Spirit" that is the real work of art and our best offering to the world. So invite this "Art Spirit" to go with you everywhere you go. I realize that some days we have less time than other days.

On the busy days of life while you are cooking, carpooling or working, you can remember to invite this spirit along for the ride. Honor it and make space for it. Invite it into every area of your life. It is the feeling we get from the activity that makes us feel good, not always the finished product.

The more you practice this, the more it will become part of your routine. Some examples of what you can do for your "Art Spirit" are below.

- Make something different for dinner
- Take a stroll and observe the colors in nature
- Go to a playground after dusk when you aren't supposed to be there - swing on a swing
- Visit a craft store
- Buy a project to create
- Set some time aside to sketch with a warm cup of tea
- Go to a new coffee shop and bring your sketchbook
- Opposite day - do things differently than you usually would - drive to work a different way, take a walk at a different place than you usually do. Shake things up a bit, because you can't do the same things and expect different results.
- Paint
- Finger paint
- Create with clay
- Try a new art medium
- Journal
- Go outside at night and look at the stars
- Go cloud watching
- Take a bath
- Visit an art museum or another type of museum
- Garden
- Sing
- Color
- Doodle

- Listen to music and dance
- Laugh
- Smile
- Wear something colorful

Time and time again when working with people, I have found that discovering the stories and the creativity thieves that have been holding us back is the key to letting go of the labels we have given ourselves around creativity. Taking the time to examine and release these stories is a pivotal part of the journey.

"A life left unexamined is not worth living."

- Socrates

#3

CREATE MOTION WITH EMOTIONS

Winter Angel

"Art is not always about pretty things. It is about who we are, what happened to us, and how our lives are affected."

- Elizabeth Brown

My white SUV was overflowing with teenage girls as I drove my daughter and her friends to the mall. They had just started experimenting with make-up, and they had some coupons for their new favorite store. They were having a conversation in the back about one of their classes and what they were learning. I was trying to block them out and enjoy the ride and the music but couldn't help but overhear their conversation.

They were learning about emotions in their health class, and they were naming emotions and the advice their teacher gave them on how to handle that particular feeling. Then they proceeded to say that their teacher said that they should never, ever feel anger.

At that point, I couldn't help myself, and I chimed in and asked, "Are you sure that is what she said?" They insisted that she told them that they should never feel anger.

By this time, we had arrived at the make-up store. After I pulled into the parking spot, I said to them, "I think it is okay to feel anger, but it is what we do with that anger that is important. We have to find ways to channel it, so we don't take it out on others. We can't deny this human emotion."

They looked at me a little a strangely at first but then began to share stories of times they were angry and what they did about it. We talked about ways we can deal with this human emotion of anger. Then they jumped out of the car and ran into the store.

As I sat in the car waiting for them, my mind flashed back to my teaching years. I remembered how everyone was so afraid to broach the topic of anger or any emotion in the schools. They had programs in the curriculum to make it look like we were dealing with emotions, but mostly everything was just swept under the rug. Most of our time was spent focusing on standardized testing.

Human Emotions

"Emotions make us human, denying them make us beasts."
- Victoria Klein

Human Emotion has always been a topic that has fascinated me. When I was a special education teacher, I spent five years teaching in an emotional support class. These kids in my class had endured more at the young age of twelve than most people deal with in a lifetime. Their experiences gave them a lot of stuff to manage emotionally. These children taught me many life lessons. One thing they helped me see was that emotions cannot be buried. When we try to hide them, we eventually blow up, have outbursts and then begin justifying the outbursts, instead of owning and releasing our emotions.

We live in such a quick-fix society, where we don't let anyone feel their feelings. Instead, we jump right to trying to fix their feelings. What if we gave people a little space and time to explore and honor all of their feelings?

In the word emotion, is the word motion. Emotions need motion; they need to move out of us. Otherwise, they stay buried in our bodies and can produce havoc on the inside, creating discomfort, disease and unhappiness. If we don't get our emotions up and out, we look to unhealthy habits such as eating and drinking to push them down further.

There are many ways to move emotions out of our body like movement, journaling and expressing ourselves. Creativity is another means to help us express our emotions.

When I taught the emotional support class, I didn't have a strict curriculum to follow like the other classes because a lot of time was spent dealing with their emotions. I had the freedom to experiment with things like meditation, teaching them kickboxing, art projects and free writing activities. I noticed when I introduced any type of art activity they all seemed to calm down.

Can art help us deal with our emotions?

I believe it can.

I believe art, whether it is writing, music, dancing or painting, is a safe place to move emotions out of our body.

Art is a place where you can safely feel your feelings and not have to deny them. You can express them, feel them and release them through a work of art. Art also creates an inner life for us, a solace, and respite from the world. Art is a place where we can look for internal approval, instead of giving our power away.

When we are creating, we become mindful and are more open to listening to our intuition. We can look at our thoughts and emotions, release them and use them to create things we want to bring into our lives.

Healing Your Stories and Wounds through Art

Quite a few years back, when I was going through a difficult time in life, I worked with an intuitive healer, Melanie Ericksen. The work I did with her was invaluable and helped me uncover the stories I needed to heal. Stories that I had buried and forgotten about came up. Melanie's gentle and safe spirit created a space where I felt safe sharing these stories. I learned from Melanie and her healing work that these stories that we bury need to be released and witnessed by others with whom we feel secure; otherwise, they stay stuck in our cells and make us sick.

While working with Melanie, I decided to turn my stories or wounds into paintings. Whenever I shared one of the paintings that I created from these stories, people were always so intrigued by them. It was as if they felt the emotion and healing that was going on behind the scenes.

Although these stories seemed painful and negative at first, I always found a positive twist to each one of them. Writing about the story, painting the story, and the work I did with Melanie helped me dig a little deeper to find the gem in each one of them. Here is one of my buried stories.

54

Finding the Light

It was 1972, I was five years old. My mom came in to kiss me good night. She ran out of the room and came back with the thermometer. Next thing I know, my dad scooped me up and put me in the back seat of his car. My fever was over 106, and they were taking me to the ER.

When we got there the staff gathered around me and immediately took me back to a room. The nurse asked my parents to wait outside the room. I overheard one of the nurses saying, "We have to get her fever down." I wanted my mom. After being poked and prodded for a while a nurse put me in a wheelchair and said, "We are taking you to another room." They were admitting me. I kept asking the nurse, "Where is my mom? Is she going to stay with me? Is she coming to the new room with me?" I was persistent with the questions. She said, "Your mom will meet you in your room a little later."

She wheeled me out of the room and to the elevator. My mom and dad stood outside the elevator as the nurse pushed me in. As the doors shut, I saw a panicked look on my mom's face. As the elevator ascended, I called out for my mom. I asked the nurse again, "Where is my mom, is she going to stay with me? Is she coming to the new room with me?" She said in a loud aggravated voice, "I told you, your mom will meet you in your room later." Her anger silenced me. She put me in an ice tent, something they used back in the 70s to help reduce your fever, and then she left. I was alone and trapped in a tent.

My mom, a devout Catholic, taught her children how to pray at a very young age, so I started praying all the prayers my mom taught me. My bed was near the window. I peeked out the tent and saw a street light right outside the window. I stayed awake all night staring at the light and waiting for my mom. The light gave me hope and so did my prayers. My mom never came that night; no one came that night. I was alone and scared wondering why the nurse lied to me.

I always like to write about the story first and then create the painting. The painting I created for this story was my view from the hospital room that night. A window with a street light outside and stars in the sky. As I was painting I was inspired to create a dozen roses in a vase under the street light. I called this painting Around the Corner, and I believe I was drawn to paint the roses to represent love. I saw the positive lesson in this story. I had this deep gratitude for the prayers my mom had taught me at a young age and that night I learned that I was never alone and that, no matter what was going on in my life, love was always present.

Around the Corner

Working with Anger

In my work as a coach I continue to help clients work through emotions with art. I remember one client who would visibly transform whenever we talked about the emotion of anger. She'd stand with her arms crossed and scowl at me and say, "I never get angry."

In one session I finally said to her, "Maybe you should get angry; it might help."

The whole conversation lightened up the energy in the room, and she laughed and said, "I guess I do get angry on the inside, but I try to bury it." She learned that it was safe to journal and paint to get her emotions out. This client enjoyed creating abstract paintings using a lot of red paint to release the anger that had built up inside of her.

Another client came to me with the belief that art was only for a select few who were creatively gifted. She shared with me her fantasies of pouring paint and a blank canvas waiting for her to create something, but she'd never had any type of art training, and so she thought it wasn't for her. This changed after a few sessions with me; she understood that we could all express ourselves creatively.

I led her through a meditation to see if she could capture a visual of an emotion that was inside her, then she could create and release this emotion through art.

We began the meditation, and at first, she didn't see anything. A voice inside her said maybe this isn't going to work. However, she waited patiently in the void and finally an image started to appear.

She saw a sphere with sharp edges covering it. The edges scared her, but she kept going. Anger then came up for her. Then she saw a black square framing the sphere. The anger was still there, but it started to feel like it was moving. I gently asked her if he wanted to let go of this anger and she said yes. I asked what she needed to do to let go of this anger.

As I was asking her this question, my client saw a red swirl in the box on top of the sphere. She described that is was moving in a counterclockwise direction. She heard the word swoosh to describe the image. She felt a lot of energy and began to see other colors. She then felt the swoosh going towards the right side of the square, breaking it open. Energy was released into the open space. She continued to see all kinds of different colors sparkle into this open space. It felt like a magical place for her. At the end of this session, she drew a thumbnail picture of what she visualized in her meditation.

My client came back for another session to create her image on canvas. She was nervous but was beginning to realize that creativity is not just something you do, it is an expression of your soul that comes through you. She shared how vulnerable she felt at the thought of creating something. But she was ready to express herself on canvas. Something that was once a fantasy for her now became a reality as she sat in front of the canvas and poured paint on her palette. She began creating what she saw in her visualization.

While painting, she described that she felt this voice inside that was judging her. I explained that this was natural, and I told her — just don't hold back. I told her to keep painting and know that it is a process, not a finished product right away. She noticed that she felt the dark voice lift and she began to have fun with it. When she finished the painting, she described that it felt like I had been the midwife for the birth of this new creation of hers. She named it Explosion of Expression.

As soon as she went home, she found a place to hang her new creation. However, her excitement slowly shifted as she felt other emotions stirring inside of her when she viewed the painting again — disgust, shame, disappointment and rejection. Bottled-up emotions had come out on the canvas.

My client wanted to call me and ask if she could fix the painting. It hung at the bottom of her stairs, so she passed it often. However, she decided not to, and she recalled that there came a moment when she stopped resisting and accepted the painting just as it was. I believe this was symbolic of her accepting her past and all that happened in her life.

She shared that it became clear to her that this painting was her soul's expression. "Some of what my soul wants to express is not pretty," she said. "The swoosh that escapes the box seems to be full of rage mixed with passion. There's been a massive wall of resistance holding in the swirling energy. But there is an explosion breaking down that wall. It breaks through to a world filled with color and wonder. The painting is not only a snapshot of me in present time, but it also holds a memory from my past and knows my future."

The fact that she was able to release these feelings on canvas helped her see the importance of feeling all of her emotions.

One might ask, "Why would you want to paint a creation that might bring up an array of bad feelings?" I say because it is better than keeping all these emotions inside. It helps us see that we are whole and have all kinds of emotions inside of us.

It is no secret that any good artist uses their emotions to create. Whether it is on canvas, a song or a story, emotions are what bond us together and makes the work appealing to others. Think of a good song; when created with emotion, it can feel as if this song was written just for you.

Working with Sadness

Sadness is another emotion we can express through art. We can use our sadness to express and create love towards others. This next story, although so heartbreaking, is a story that I hold dear to my heart.

Several years ago, one of my college friend's daughter died suddenly from the flu. Her daughter was an outgoing, funny and spirited kindergarten student who loved ladybugs. So much so that at her funeral, she was dressed in a ladybug dress and ladybug stockings.

The loss of a child is one of the most painful experiences a human can endure. There are no words or actions that can take the pain away. We can only offer our love and gestures of our love. When I came home from the funeral, I had so many emotions and feelings about my friend's loss; I didn't know what to do with them. I couldn't sleep because I was thinking of her and this hardship she was facing. The next day, I knew I needed to do something with these emotions, so I ordered an Eastern Redbud tree to be sent to her so she could plant it in her daughter's memory. Then I sat down in my studio to create a spring painting to go along with it. I painted some water because they loved the beach and added a bench and a spring tree with her daughter's initials carved in the tree. I wanted to add an angel to the painting. I took the painting to my art class and shared it with Karl. I asked him where he would suggest adding the angel; I thought maybe an angel cloud would work. He pointed to the leaves in my tree and said it looks as though you created an angel shape in the tree with the leaves and you didn't even realize it. We looked at the tree in stunned silence and then I added some paint to emphasize the angel a little more. I mailed it to my friend; she was touched by the gesture.

Months passed and the holiday season was upon us; I couldn't quite fathom what my friend must have been going through with the first Christmas approaching. I decided to create another painting for her. The idea came to me, and it flowed through me quickly. I painted a snow scene with little footprints leading up to a tree and an angel on top of the tree. There was also a bunny, a deer and a cardinal in the picture.

It was the beginning of December when I was working on this painting and when I finished it, out of nowhere a ladybug landed on the top right corner of the canvas. I couldn't believe it. I was painting with a friend, and she quickly took out her phone and captured a photo of the ladybug on the painting. After she snapped the picture, the ladybug flew away.

I mailed the painting, which I named *I Am Not Far*, along with a copy of the photo with the ladybug to my college friend. My friend wrote to me and said that in this time of deep sadness she could look at the painting and it brought a smile to her face. She knew it was her daughter.

I knew it was her daughter too. Years later, I went to a medium with a friend, and this little girl came through and acknowledged the paintings and thanked me for creating them for her mom.

As I was gathering information for this chapter on emotions, it popped into my mind to write about this ladybug story. I put it on my list to reach out to my friend that day and ask her permission to share this story in my book. Before I had a chance to do so, I received a message from my friend. She said that today her daughter would have been thirteen years old. She also thanked me for the book I sent her, as a few months prior I had donated one of my children's books (which has a ladybug character in it) to a special section in the school library that was in honor of her daughter. She said thank you, and she knew her daughter was smiling down from heaven on both of us. I had just finished taking a walk when I received her message. I felt so moved and had full-body chills, I had to take a few minutes to sit down on a nearby bench. There was no doubt in both of our minds that her daughter orchestrated this whole event on what would have been her thirteenth birthday.

I Am Not Far

I have always believed that when our loved ones leave us physically, they are still around us. This painting and experience was proof to me that our loved ones in heaven are not far away and that they are always communicating with us and giving us messages.

Activities

Below are some ways that you can use your emotions to create. Give them a try; it is so much healthier than reaching for food or alcohol to fill the void. All these unhealthy habits cause inflammation in our body which can lead to all types of disease. Not to mention when we stuff our angry and sad emotions, we can keep ourselves from our happy and joyful emotions, thereby living our lives in a catatonic state.

Express yourself creatively and get healthy and happy at the same time!

1. Create Something in Honor of a Life- Changing Event

When a life-changing event is coming up for you or your family, use this opportunity to create something. When my daughter left for college last year, it was such a bittersweet time for me. I thought she was going to a college nearby, but she wound up at a place that was over four hours away. Well, out of nowhere this hit me, and I couldn't stop crying. My son looked at me one day and said half joking, "Do you think maybe you need therapy?" It made me chuckle, for I knew a little art therapy was order. I had to do something with these overwhelming emotions I was feeling, so I used these feelings to create.

I wrote a blog post about my daughter leaving, I wrote her a poem, and I created a painting she could hang in her dorm. I felt like a little piece of me was going off to college with her. This painting I did for my daughter's dorm was a painting of the college she would be attending. I did a purple sky, because that is one of the school colors, and a popular building at the University with trees surrounding it. I painted college kids milling about the campus with her and her roommate in the foreground. We made copies and she gives them out to her friends. I donated a few to a school function and they auctioned off for much more than they were worth. It is the gift that keeps giving.

2. Move the Emotion of Anger Out of Your Body

When you are feeling the emotion of anger, I suggest the first step is to accept it and then do some type of movement. Dance or exercise, swing on a swing, take a walk or a run. Then sit down and journal about what you are feeling, write a letter or paint a painting. I have found that abstract pictures are great for expressing anger. Pouring paint and moving it around the canvas freely feels good. I have also discovered that some of my best paintings come from this because I am not controlling the painting, I am expressing.

*Please note, if you have continued anger issues, it is best to seek the help of a trained professional.

3. Create in Memory of a Loved One

Create something in memory of a loved one who is no longer here in the physical world. This can help with the overwhelming emotions because you move these emotions out when creating your painting, story or sculpture, etc. This activity will help you feel like your loved ones are even closer to you, and they might also give you messages while you are creating.

4. Turn Your Childhood Stories or Wounds into Creations

If there is a story that needs healing from childhood, perhaps it is a story that came up in the previous chapter around your creativity thieves. You can create something to help you clear the story. You can express your emotions around this story in a painting or a poem or a song. The more I did this activity, the more compassionate I became towards others, recognizing that everyone has stories they need to release. All of us have problems we are struggling with on a daily basis. As I created the painting of the view from the hospital room, I realized that maybe the nurse who silenced me that night was tired and at the end of her shift and didn't feel like listening to a scared child who had a lot of questions. Maybe she was having family problems. Who knows? All I do know, is that after creating that painting I could leave the painful part of this story behind.

5. Paint When You Are Feeling Happy

Using any kind of emotion to create makes it more meaningful. Sure, sadness and anger might make the creation more vulnerable and healing, but we can also take advantage of our happy times to create and get into the flow. We can use our happy emotions to create and paint what we love. We can also use this state of flow to work on planning future projects. Your paintings become your diary, and when we paint what we love and want to create in our lives we bring ourselves into a higher vibration. More on this topic when you learn about Creative Way #7 - Be Bold - Be Brave - Be You!

"A work of art which did not begin in emotion is not art."

- Paul Cezanne

#4
HOW TO SURRENDER AND TAKE INSPIRED ACTION

Moondchild

"God, grant me the serenity to accept the things I cannot change,

Courage to change the things I can,

And wisdom to know the difference."

- Reinhold Niebuhr

When I was a teenager, this prayer hung in our powder room; my mom loved this prayer, and she proudly displayed it for all to see. The words, printed on top of a bold sunset in white lettering, caught my attention every time I stepped foot in the powder room. I either read the poem or looked at the visual and pondered the meaning. Often feeling confused about what I could change or control and what I couldn't change or control, I began an inner quest to find these answers.

In observing myself and the clients I have worked with, I have noticed that most of us spend a lot of time and energy trying to control things that we have no control over and then we have no energy left for the things we can control in our lives. So much of our life is spent worrying about people, things and situations we have no control over.

I think knowing the difference between what we can and cannot control is the hard part. Our society programs us to work hard, to keep moving and to push, push, push! This never allows for time to get quiet and listen and find peace. But there is this other way of living that is so much easier; it is about going with the flow and drifting downstream, instead of continually trying to push against the stream. It's about tuning in to one's intuition.

I think all of us have experienced a glimmer of this at some point in our lives. For example, did you ever lose something and, like a crazy person, spend a lot of energy looking everywhere for it? Tired, you finally give in and accept that you can't find it and move on to something else. Then all of a sudden, it pops in your mind where to look for the lost item. You look, and it is there. This is surrender, and most of the time we don't even realize we are doing it.

How would it feel to live like this all the time?

Would you like to let go of worry and see the big picture?

Living without trying to control everything and everyone around you isn't about being passive; it is about surrendering and taking the right inspired actions. There are things in life that we can't control, and when we get quiet and know the difference, we are led to the right actions.

This inner quest to understand surrender led me to a variety of books on the topic of surrender and intuition. After my "paint or drink heavily" incident,

The *Bill W.* book (the absorbing and deeply moving life story of Bill Wilson, co-founder of Alcoholics Anonymous) found its way into my hands. This book taught me about surrender and being of service. I also learned from this book that it is important to listen to the message and not the messenger. Put your power in the message, not the person; they are human and there is no need to put anyone on a pedestal.

In 2011, I came across a book called *Outrageous Openness - Letting the Divine take the Lead* by Tosha Silver. This title says it all. The book came in the mail and I opened it and read it in one sitting. Next thing you know I was signing up for Tosha's classes. Suddenly the prayer that caught my attention as a teenager made perfect sense to me. It was like some profound mystery that I had reflected on for years was solved. Tosha's work was the missing piece that made me grasp this concept more fully.

My fascination with this inner guidance system or intuition that I was curious about since I was a teenager dialed up a notch.

Our intuition or our inner guidance system always knows the right answer, but we have our shadow voice that chimes in and creates confusion and makes it difficult to hear our intuitive voice. When we do hear this intuitive voice we often ignore it. We go around asking other people their opinions rather than going inside ourselves to find the answers.

In this world with its increasing distractions we are surrounded by people who want to give us advice. One of the problems with this is they are giving us information based on their stories, their feelings and their judgments. Many times these people want the best for us, and the advice is well intended. However, it is not always the right advice for us.

We too are probably guilty of doing this same thing with our friends and family members. Many of us go around projecting our experiences on others and think everyone should follow the path we are on. We believe that if it worked for us, it will work for others.

A few years back, my one friend who had been married for years was giving dating advice to another friend and insisting she knew what was best, even though she had not been on a date in years. Her advice was that you should go on three dates with someone before you make a decision about the person, which is a rule she created back when she was dating. But what if your intuition told you within five minutes of the first date that this didn't feel right? Then what? Do you force yourself to go on two more dates?

This "advice-giving" conversation can get us into the comparing game, which gets us nowhere and often leaves both parties feeling bad. It can zap our energy and make us feel drained, leaving us no time for the things we want to do in our life. I observed my friends as they were conversing about the "three-date rule" and the friend who was dating started to doubt herself out loud, stating that maybe she didn't give people a chance and that maybe she should be nicer like our three- date rule" friend. "I can be stubborn," she said. It seemed like she was putting herself down when she said this. Then she stated things that made her feel uncomfortable about the guy she had gone on the first date with. I could tell this was her intuition speaking. I finally chimed in and said, "I think this rule is ridiculous!" We all laughed and agreed that maybe the three-date rule isn't for everyone.

How can we avoid these conversations?

Maybe by listening to others before offering our input; listening helps us tune into our intuition. When we take the time to tune into our intuition we realize that guidance is unique for each of us and there is no one-size-fits-all answer.

Listening to your Intuition

From years of teaching special education, I saw the importance of teaching kids how to listen to their intuition because each learner was different. A learning strategy that worked for one child didn't work for another. Like I said, I loved this topic of intuition and was always searching for ways to listen to my inner guidance. In addition to reading books, I took countless classes on intuition over the years.

When I had my children, I knew I wanted to teach them about more than just their five senses; I desired to teach them about the most important sense of all - their intuition.

First, I taught them what intuition was or felt like. I showed them how to listen to their intuition or their gut, which some call our second brain. I explained to them what intuition was —a feeling you get inside as to what actions to take. But first you have to spend time listening and just being. I explored different kinds of meditation and taught them about meditation. However, I must be honest: I have such high energy that I often had a hard time sitting still to meditate.

I didn't just fill my children with answers and information; I encouraged them to listen to their inner guidance. Listening helped them see that their answers and the information/knowledge they needed or desired were within them. In my experience, I have noticed that children grasp this concept fairly easy but adults seem to struggle with it. We are so used to looking to someone else for answers, or praying and talking about our problems, that we rarely make any time to stop, get quiet, and listen to our intuition that guides us to the right answers and actions.

I taught my kids to talk to God and the angels when they were concerned or worried about something. I told them to ask God and be patient and listen. Sometimes He didn't answer right away, and sometimes their answers came from another person, an experience, or in their dreams. I told them to look for signs in nature. I also explained to them how to listen to their bodies. Sometimes I felt like teaching them about their intuition was like teaching a whole new language, the language of Spirit.

My daughter would sometimes look at me and say, "But you're the mom, you are the one that is supposed to give me the answer. What should I do? Tell me." I would have conversations with her as to what was going on but deeply felt that, unless it was my intuition urging me to give her an answer, it was best for me to encourage her to listen to her intuition. I knew I wasn't always going to be there to give her an answer so I felt that teaching my children about their intuition was one of the best gifts I could give them.

Although I was happy with how I taught my children about their intuition, I still struggled with making a connection between my intuition and meditation. As I mentioned earlier, I explored all different types of meditation. I took classes on being mindful, practiced yoga, enrolled in specific meditation courses, listened to CDs and even read books on meditation. Sure, I found some good techniques that relaxed me, but the feeling never seemed to last. I desired more. I wanted answers … a knowing, a deeper connection and purpose while meditating.

While I was trying to piece this all together I was introduced to this amazing concept. The Institute for Integrative Nutrition® teaches the term "bio-individuality", which is the concept that no one diet or lifestyle works for everyone. Each person's nutritional needs are individual and based on a number of varying factors such as lifestyle, occupation, climate, age, gender, culture, and religion. Lifestyle needs are individual as well; what works for one person may not work for another with regard to relationships, exercise, career, spirituality, and physical activity. Additionally, people's needs change over time, so it is important to check in with yourself as you evolve.

How we meditate is something that is unique to the individual and also changes over time. After this, I started exploring more ways to meditate and ways to listen to my intuition. I was searching for a way to meditate that worked for me and didn't feel forced. Sitting still for too long didn't work for me. I needed a quicker way to meditate because, when life got busy, it felt too overwhelming to carve out long periods of time. I longed to be present, instead of jumping to the next thought and not enjoying the experience I was having.

Over time my friend and I came up with a meditation I am going to share with you now. It is called Inspired Action Meditation, and it helps you to find that inner place of stillness and knowing.

What is Inspired Action Meditation?

This technique evolved slowly over the period of a few years. My friend and I were in our forties and this way of discovering how to be present and meditate helped us with what she calls our mid-life reconstruct, that time when you feel like there is something more to life, when you realize some of the old ways you knew and patterns you had aren't working anymore.

We started Inspired Action because meditation was challenging for us; both of us had such high energy that we had a hard time quieting our minds and found it challenging to be still for a long time.

We came up with a way to silence our shadow voice by focusing on a particular issue at hand and then together we would listen for the guidance of our intuition. We lived over 3,000 miles apart so we would do this meditation via phone or Skype.

We tapped into our imaginations and intuitions and discovered messages that came from the universe, angels, our guides and ancestors. We would receive images, words, stories and songs for each other as we meditated. Sometimes the messages we got made no sense to us, but it made sense to the other when we shared it. We slowly learned how to trust these messages. We realized it was no longer our shadow voice trying to control the situation or give advice from our positions. We listened and tuned into this higher power and shared it with each other.

Meditating with two or more people is powerful. Inspired Action Meditation feels good because we are helping others and getting help at the same time. If a friend or family member is having a particularly difficult situation, we both focus on one person's issue. Inspired Action helps us decipher the difference between our intuition and our shadow voice, and it helps us sit back and be a witness to our thoughts.

In the beginning, my friend would have lots of doubts about her messages, and she would say things like, "I think I got that message because I just saw something like that in a movie." She was nervous that it wasn't her intuition but her imagination. It was at this time we delved deeper into our meditation and began to understand that the answers are all around us and within us. Our imagination is one source, and our dreams are another. The shadow voice throws doubt and wants to control. Keeping this controlling voice in check is essential, and asking our guides, ancestors and angels to come in and be present to guide us is vital in the process.

How to Use Inspired Action

"For whenever two or more of you are gathered

in His name, there is Love."

- Matthew 18:20

Find a buddy and use Inspired Action with them so that you can align your-self with inspired actions. I have several and also have taught my kids how to use it. I also use it with my clients to help them seek answers to things they are struggling with.

Inspired Action is done with at least one other person but can also be done in a group. As you start to do it with others you will find that you can also use these steps on your own when you need guidance.

It is best to be done with someone you feel safe with; a trusted confidant, a soul friend or someone from your tribe. You must feel free and comfortable so you can share your struggles, open to other dimensions, let go and relax. This meditation is a place of genuine surrender.

Remember, if a friend or family member is having a particularly difficult situation, you both focus and meditate on the one person's issue.

The Steps for Inspired Action

"The best teachers [and friends] are those who show you where to look

but don't tell you what to see."

- Alexandra K. Trenfor

Step 1 - Create a Place to Meditate Where You Feel Comfortable

This place is unique for everyone. I sometimes feel comfortable using Inspired Action Meditation while I walk, paint or cook; other times I sit in a chair in my office I use for meditation. My friend likes to sit in the same place in her house when she does Inspired Action Meditation. She always lights a candle and puts on background music for us. There are no strict rules as to where or how to sit, and we have found that when we take away the rules we can tune into our intuition easier because there is no pressure.

Step 2 - Say a Prayer together

My friend and I created some prayers we say together that call in God, the angels our guides and ancestors. We call on special loved ones who have gone before us. Even though they aren't here in the physical form, we can feel them around us, especially when we meditate. We each created our own altar where we have pictures of these ancestors. I have a photo of my paternal grandfather and maternal grandmother. We also have pictures of angels and ascended masters we feel are special to us. I have a picture of Jesus and Archangel Michael and a statue of Mother Mary. A hand-drawn picture of Vincent Van Gogh and a Wayne Dyer book also sit on my altar to guide me with my painting and writing. We change our altars periodically and have also decorated them with other items such as crystals, fresh flowers, etc.

Here is one of the prayers that we created.

Dear God, Ancestors, Angels, Guides and Ascended Masters,

Please help us surrender so we can listen to our intuition, which we know is really you guiding us. We give you all our worries, concerns, struggles and also our desires. We let go so that something magical can happen. We know when we let go we give you room to do your work. Then we can listen to the actions we need to take. Let us be of service to you. Let us do your work in the world. Amen.

We have also used the Marianne Williamson's book *Illuminata: A Return to Prayer;* it is a good resource because it has prayers for specific topics such as relationships, family, addictions and other struggles.

Step 3 - State or Express a Purpose for Meditation

State what is bothering you or what you need help or guidance with. During this time, we take time to share things that are going well in our lives, our desires and also our struggles, and it helps us clarify our purpose for meditation. Quite often we have found that our desires are related to our struggles. We then take the time to set our purpose in a clear statement. For example: Guides and Angels, please give me guidance as to the next step I should take with my business.

We have also found that Inspired Action Meditation can be very helpful to use for asking questions about food, exercise or health.

Step 4 - Begin the Meditation

Take two deep breaths and then sit quietly for at least three to five minutes and be present. We sometimes sit longer. We listen for any messages that may come in the form of words, songs, feelings, stories, etc. Let whatever happens come and don't try to control the experience. I have found that some people I use Inspired Action Meditation with like to have a journal with them to write things down. Remember it is a unique experience for each person.

Step 5 - Share the Messages You Received in Meditation

Just share what you get. Don't try to control and change the message, only share it. It is coming from a higher source and might not make sense to you but might make perfect sense to the other person. Anything you receive in this meditation is something to share, even if it is one of your stories. You will be pleasantly surprised by the honesty and freedom during this time. If you receive an inspired action that might be right for the other person during meditation, gently offer the suggestions. You can help guide the person in making a plan to take that action if it feels right to them. This step can be challenging at times because now you are back in the present time and the shadow voice can come into play.

We have discovered that an action that might seem so easy for one person takes a lot of bravery for another person, so we guide each other to feel the fear and do it anyway.

For example, one time my friend received the message that it was time for me to let go of an instructor I had for my children for years. She said it like it was so easy to do. I started defending the teacher even though this person was draining my energy and taking advantage of me. There was a huge part of me that just didn't want to be bothered with letting her go. I just wanted to go along with it and not rock the boat. I had a fear of letting her go. My friend helped me make a plan and set a time that I would do it. My knees were shaking and I felt so bad doing it, but I did it. I was glad I had her to hold me accountable and guide me with this action that gave me my energy back.

Sometimes the inspired action we receive in meditation is to take no action with a particular situation, and to surrender just a bit more.

After we finish the meditation, we always take the time to thank God, our guides and our ancestors.

Step 6 - Look for Signs After Meditation

This quiet time opens you up to receiving more messages, so pay attention to these messages. Sometimes the message happened instantly and other times they happened later that day or days following the meditation. My friend and I noticed that we always received messages that related to our meditation. These messages are often filled with serendipity and we were often blown away by some of the signs. For example, we would hear a song on the radio that we received in meditation or get a call from someone out of the blue that wanted to do business with us, receive messages in our dreams, get something in the mail or see a sign on the highway related to the messages we received in mediation. We would get answers to the questions we asked in meditation.

On one occasion, I was meditating with my son. His question for the mediation was he wanted to know if he should go to a party he was invited to. It was at a restaurant and he needed to RSVP that night. He was concerned because he wasn't sure if he was going to know anyone at the party. I suggested he ask his friends if they were going. He said he felt bad asking because he didn't know who was invited (since the person having the party wasn't in their friend group). We meditated for guidance. Not too long after our meditation, one of his friends texted him and asked him if he was going to the party. He sighed a breath of relief and had his answer.

Remember, listening to our intuition is like learning a different language; the messages can come in so many different ways and forms. A song, a conversation, a book or a book title, a feeling, a person. Sometimes the answers come instantly in meditation or right after; and other times the universe has work to do behind the scenes. It is important to trust the process and the mystery.

Inspired Action Meditation taps you into this inner world and helps you to see things clearly and from a higher perspective. It is something we can carry with us into all areas of life. It connects us to other dimensions because it keeps us open as we look for signs and messages.

With Inspired Action Meditation in our lives we learn how to act instead of constantly reacting to situation we have little or no control over. It encourages us to take powerful inspired action that helps us live meaning and fulfilling lives.

Other activities you can implement into your life to help you surrender and take Inspired Action:

1. Listen to Your Body

If we get quiet and stay still long enough, our bodies will give us the answer. I learned this technique in a class I took on intuition. We had to think of something where we knew the answer was a yes, for example: My name is Christine and I have two children. We then were encouraged to still our minds and settle into our physical beings to see where we felt this truth in our bodies. I felt my yes in my stomach. It is a movement that starts at the bottom of my stomach and moves up. Next, you had to think of a question where you knew the answer was a no. Again, the instruction was to get quiet and search out where we felt this answer in our bodies. I felt my no in my neck and shoulder area. It started in my neck and moved down my shoulders. When I feel this in my body, I know it is an indication for me to say no to a situation.

Last year, my daughter graduated high school and her senior year was spent applying for colleges and waiting to hear back from them. Then decision time came, and in the end, she made her decision by using her inner guidance and the feeling she felt in her body. I'd taught her this yes and no activity when she was younger.

She had received a scholarship to one university, so naturally, she thought that would be a good choice. However, when she visited this school, she described that she felt this depressed, slumpy feeling every time she was on the campus. She knew that she felt her no on her shoulders. Even though she felt the answer was a no, she kept trying to convince herself to go there because of the scholarship. We visited this college several times, and every time she felt this same heaviness. She shared her feelings with me, and we decided it wasn't a good idea for her to go there. She then went back to her acceptance list and decided to visit a college she had applied to but never visited. As soon as she set foot on the campus, she felt this feeling of movement in her feet that made her want to explore. Since she feels her yes in her feet, she felt confident that this school could be a good choice.

It brings a smile to my face when she sends me photos of her and her friends hiking in the trails and mountains that are nearby.

A perfect fit for some is not suitable for others.

2. Ground Yourself

Go outside and walk barefoot on the earth, put your feet in mud. Lay your whole body down on the grass. Grounding yourself is a great activity to do before, during or after Inspired Action Meditation.

Eat grounding foods that grow deep in the earth - root vegetables such as carrots, potatoes, sweet potatoes or winter squash. Or grind root spices such as ginger and turmeric and use them in hot drinks and as you cook. Notice the difference in your body as you eat them, feel the energy of these foods. I share one of my favorite grounding soup recipes later on in the book.

3. Create a God Box or Angel Box

Get a box for this activity - you can either go to your local craft store and purchase a box or you can make a box by covering and decorating an old shoebox. Place this box in a special place in your home. Then write your worries and/or desires on a small piece of paper and place them in the box. I taught my children this ritual when they were young and I have been doing this activity myself for years. This act helps you release because you are surrendering the things that are controlling you, whether it be a worry or something you want to bring into your life over to God. You get a feeling inside like ah, I am giving this to God, so it is no longer mine to worry about. This is a gift to ourselves and everyone around us. It enables us to be present for ourselves and for those we love. The physical act of putting these struggles in a box helps us reduce worry and keeps us from being distracted. My kids and I experienced a feeling of lightness time and time again once we handed over these concerns to God.

You can also have a ritual of periodically cleaning out your God box by burning the pieces of paper in your box or by getting rid of them in some way.

4. Use Angel Cards for Guidance

There are many Angels Cards available today for you to choose from. Keep a deck nearby to help guide you. You can ask a question in the morning and pick a card for guidance. You can also pick a card after your Inspired Action Meditation. Before going to bed is also an excellent time to ask for guidance. Some answers may come to you in your dreams. Some of the decks you might be interested in are Doreen Virtue Angel card decks. She has a lot of different decks and I have several of them. I also like Colette Baron-Reid's decks, and The Wisdom of the Oracle are my favorite. She also has many different decks. You can also get a professional angel card reading done for further guidance.

5. Another Ritual to Help You Stop Worrying

Worry is an emotion that can take hold of us out of nowhere. Worry projects into the future and is not a present reality. Most of the times when we are worrying there usually isn't anything we can do about the worry in the present moment. It can be exhausting. I created this ritual many years ago when my kids were little. I created it to help release worry and enjoy the moment. Here is how I came up with the idea.

One day my daughter was pushing her younger brother on the swing in our backyard. As I watched them, I felt a pull to go inside and clean up the kitchen but instead sat down on the warm grass and watched my children play.

The big, puffy clouds caught my attention and next thing you know we were playing the cloud game, one of our favorites. It was moments like this that made me feel like I didn't have a worry in the world, but I must admit in a drop of a hat I could go to the extreme opposite place. That crazy place of endless fear and creating scenarios in my mind.

The cloud game didn't last long; next thing you know my son jumped up and was climbing up the high part of the swing set. "Be careful; that is really high!" He didn't listen to a word I said; he just kept climbing higher and higher. As I was frantically telling him to stop, a puffy cloud caught my attention; it looked like an angel. I thought to myself, "Why am I wasting so much time worrying? It is exhausting!" At that moment an idea for a painting popped into my mind.

That night I went to my studio and started painting as if it were an assignment from God and the angels. Most of the time when I start a painting, I only have a loose idea and then I let the rest come to me as I paint. So with the idea of my children surrounded by angels, I began the painting. When I was done, I had a night sky with a full moon, my children sitting on a grassy hill covered with moonflowers under the stars, and a tree to their left. In the sky, I added two angel clouds. A new painting was born that day and a new ritual.

I have this painting displayed in a place where I can look at it when I wake up. Every morning I stop and say a prayer and visualize my children protected by angels. It only takes a few minutes. Anytime I worry ... I repeat the prayer and visualize the painting.

Here are three easy steps to help you create your ritual

Step 1

Create something to help you visualize this ritual of being worry-free. Create a collage of your kids, a painting a drawing or use your imagination and come up with your own creation. Let your intuition guide you. I am using worrying about our kids as an example. However, you can create a symbol for whatever your topic of worry might be.

Step 2

Make an altar in a special place in your home - on it put the creation you made that represents your children or another worry. Then you can add other items, such as statues of angels, crystals, fresh flowers. Here is your chance to tap into your creativity. Visit the altar when you wake up and say a prayer to protect your children. My prayer is simple and only takes a minute to say.

Here is the prayer.

Dear God and the Angels –

Please watch over my children as they go out into this great big world. Wrap your loving arms around them and protect them. Thank you and Amen.

Step 3

Throughout the day if you feel worried, go back to this protection prayer for your child. If you are home, you can visit the altar or you can take a photo of it so you have the visual altar on your phone.

As my children grew and reached different milestones, like getting their driver's permit and license, I found myself looking at the painting and saying the prayer more and more. It gave me peace and complete surrender. In that moment I felt love instead of fear. As we know, there are no guarantees in this life; it is a mystery. But one thing I learned for sure is worrying is wasted energy and keeps us from the present moment.

When my daughter left for college, the painting remained in the same spot and every day even though she is miles away, I continue the ritual that I started many years ago and deep in my heart I know I am inviting her angels to go with her. When we moved her into her dorm, I gave her a print of the painting in hopes that she will carry on this ritual and turn to surrender instead of worry and fear. In every moment we have a choice: we can either choose worry and fear or love and surrender.

Moonlight Angels

"On the other side of that veil, there are angels riding with their chariots of fire to be a protection for your child."

- Elder Jeffrey R. Holland

The intuitive voice is the calm, grounded voice we hear inside. The shadow voice is all about drama, problems and believes there is never enough. I guarantee with practice you will get to know the difference.

Quite often the shadow voice makes an even louder appearance when we sit down to create. These thoughts like "you are not good enough" or "you can't create" can make us want to avoid and run away from creativity. Instead of judging these dark thoughts we can use these moments as an opportunity to befriend this shadow voice so it isn't running the show.

Social Programming is all about control, but having the inner strength to listen to the wisdom inside you can free you from some of this programming. Since the programming is all about the external world and how things look on the outside, we can become programmed to worry about the opinions of others.

This is a lifelong journey. The more you practice listening to the intuitive voice and not judging your shadow voice, the more you will be able to free yourself from caring about what other people think of you and your life. You will open wide the door to your creative endeavors.

#5
PRACTICE SELF-CARE WITH A SPIN

The Fire Within

"Before enlightenment chop wood, carry water.

After enlightenment chop wood, carry water."

- Zen Proverb

I glance at the clock. OH NOOOOOO!!!!!

5:00 pm, already?

Where did the day go?

I dreamed of getting so much done today. But no, it was another day of not getting anything done, I thought as I reached into the kids' candy stash.

Sure, I did some things …

I met a friend for a walk and had to listen to all of her problems. She complained the whole hour and a half we walked. I wanted to scream and say, "Suck it up, we all have issues." But I smiled, listened and offered her little bits of advice. I don't even think she heard.

Then I went home, made the kids' lunch and felt so burned out. I wanted to paint, but instead I took a nap.

I woke up, made cookies for the event at school and now the entire day is almost gone, and nothing I wanted to do got accomplished.

I wanted to take an Epsom salt bath, write the bills that are late, paint and just sit in front of the fire and journal, but I didn't do any of this and I am so frustrated.

Now back to work tomorrow!

I can't have another Sunday like this.

Now I have to make dinner, and I have no energy.

> *I should have woken up earlier this morning!*
>
> *Frustrated, I start screaming at the kids and then head to the pantry and start eating anything I can get my hands on. I am starving! I never sat down to eat lunch.*
>
> *I am on a hamster wheel.*
>
> *Same old stuff, different day.*
>
> *How do I change this?*
>
> *Help!*

Does this sound familiar? I think all of us have been here at one time or another, especially moms. The above story is from one of my clients, and I am happy to say that she has come a long way with changing her schedule and owning her life.

When we hear someone else's story like this one, we could probably quickly give our two cents on how to change it. Wake up earlier, get the junk food out of your house, say no to the draining friend and volunteering to make cookies. But it is easier said than done when it comes to our own lives and how we practice self-care.

What Exactly is Self-care Anyway?

Here is my spin on it.

It is a hot topic consuming a large section of the bookstore lately. When we hear the word self-care, I think many of us dream up visions of relaxing salt baths, dark chocolate and taking time to dream of the future.

After working with clients and after years of doing inner work, I came up with this spin on self-care — my definition. Here it is: I believe self-care is about taking the whole person into consideration. It is about accepting the good and bad in life and also accepting our strengths and our weaknesses. It is about embracing and honoring all of our feelings and not pushing away any feelings that might not feel good to us. When we deny our feelings, we tend to overindulge in things that bring us pleasure and avoid the things we need to do in order to feel whole. Overindulging is a temporary fix, only making us feel even worse afterward. Self-care is about enjoying pleasures while facing the tasks we might want to run and hide from. We feel good about ourselves when we do that thing we are afraid to do — that thing our intuitive voice gently guides us to do. Self-care is about showing up and feeling at peace no matter what we are doing or what is going on in our lives. It is about embracing your unique journey and finding your purpose.

Sometimes I think we are led to believe, or we have this fantasy inside, that someday someone is just going to come along and save us and magically do our everyday tasks for us.

Nothing can be further from the truth because even if someone did come along we probably still wouldn't be satisfied. A big part of self-care is practicing how to be mindful while doing our everyday so-called mundane tasks. We are all given the same twenty-four hours in a day. It is up to us how we choose to spend our time.

Making boundaries and selecting activities that make us happy and feel fulfilled is key to self-care. Maybe this client could have made the cookies after she had done things for herself. If she woke up and did the items on the list that she wanted to get done, like taking a bath and writing out her bills that were late, she would have been in a much better place for herself and her family.

Self-care is also about doing things we don't want to do, like taking a look at our finances or showing up for a creative endeavor instead of distracting ourselves with food and other things. I like to call this is grown-up self-care. In working with my clients, I have found that their lives are balanced and work well when they intermingle the Epsom salt baths, dark chocolate, and lattes with grown-up self-care like finances and other daily tasks we all tend to resist.

Creativity can be a tricky one; it can go on both lists because sometimes we so want to do it and other times we avoid it. Oftentimes when we sit down to create, our shadow voice shows up big and strong. So instead of facing and embracing this shadow voice, we avoid it altogether. When we face the shadow voice and accept it, our lives are so much easier.

Here is a snippet of how my client and I worked on her issues around self-care.

I listened to her and asked her lots of open-ended questions, such as: What do you want to spend your time doing? Why do you feel like you are on a hamster wheel? How can you change this? How do you feel when your bills are late? This helped her get clear and helped her come up with answers that were inside of her.

We practiced Inspired Action Meditation so she could go within and get straight on what she wanted and get guidance from her inner self and God. Through the meditation process she gained clarity on what she wanted to do with her life: She wanted to create a business so she could eventually leave her job and be her own boss.

This client was a big dreamer who avoided practical tasks. She needed grounding and needed to have her actions broken down into small steps like most of us do. I have found that highly creative people put way too much on their list and they go into overload. The expression "make a list and cut it in half" always came to mind when I worked with her. She had to brain dump her long list to get it out in her journal and then she could look and see what was humanly possible. We created a unique journal for her that met her needs. (There is a sample of this journal at the end of this chapter.)

Back in the 90s, when I was teaching, I went to a workshop on how to be productive. The main thing I learned at the workshop was that to be productive you should do the least favorite job on your list first. I have found that going right to the job I resist the most and getting it done frees up my energy. We spend so much time and energy procrastinating on the things we don't want to do; however, when we do the job we resist first, a kind of magic takes place inside and we become more productive. When we do the things we oppose early in the morning — whether it be exercise or your bills— it's as if the unconscious mind isn't even awake yet so you aren't even aware that you are doing something you don't like. This strategy worked very well for my client.

We worked on meal planning so she was prepared ahead of time with healthy go-to treats, instead of always reaching for unhealthy treats. We will get into this in the next chapter. We integrated both nurturing self-care and grown-up self-care into her life (see the list on the next page).

She learned how to celebrate the small steps towards her goal – we called these her triumphs — while she simultaneously thought of her next steps. She learned how to face things that didn't work for her on a particular day or things she would do differently. We called these her tribulations. Accepting her tribulations took some time because she quite often denied or defended the actions that weren't working for her. She often went from beating herself up when she faced her tribulations to stopping her actions when she celebrated her triumphs. She learned to accept both triumphs and tribulations and saw herself as a work in progress. The combination of consciously allowing both our triumphs and tribulations in our life is a happy place for most, I have found.

She learned to say no and learned how to set boundaries by saying, "I can't make the cookies until I get take a bath and pay the bills." Prioritizing worked perfectly for her. It enabled her to get her task completed more efficiently. She had to stop saying yes when she meant no, which was tough for her. She spent most of her life people pleasing. But as an adult, this obviously wasn't working for her anymore. She needed a plan so she could feel good about her life. She took small steps and after some time she went from feeling frustrated, over-weight and unhappy to feeling fulfilled and nourished in her life. With this new way of living, she looked forward to waking up in the morning because she tapped into her passions and desires. This benefited her and her family.

Activities

Are you ready to implement a self-care routine into your life? Below are activities to help you get started. The activities are followed by some self-care recipes and rituals.

1. Grown-up Self-care and Nurturing Self-care
Part of Your Everyday Life

Below is a list of grown-up self-care and nurturing self-care for you to choose from, and remember to intermingle the two! You can add more items to the list. Remember that this is a unique experience for everyone. What is considered joyful to one can be drudgery to another.

Grown-up Self-care

- Putting time in your calendar to tend to your money issues — paying bills, budgeting, etc.
- Doing the thing on your list that you don't want to do first
- Say no
- Laundry
- Cleaning
- Planning healthy meals
- Saving money by making your meals at home instead of going out to eat
- Carve out time for creativity by writing it on your calendar
- Get started on that book you have been dreaming about for years; just take one small step today and then another and another

Nurturing Self-care

- Light some candles and take an Epsom salt bath
- Journal
- Treat yourself to dark chocolate
- Time in nature
- Carve out time for creativity
- Go to the coffee shop and bring a book or a journal
- Read before you go to bed
- Sit in front of a fire and dream of the future
- Get pedicure or manicure

- Use essential oils
- Dry brushing
- Make a homemade face mask
- Practice yoga
- Practice face yoga
- Oil Pulling (I love doing this but have found this goes on the grown-up self-care for some)
- Use an Epsom salt scrub in the shower
- Laugh out loud

2. Designate a Day for Each Task that You Resist Doing

Here is an example of some of mine -

- Money Monday or Finance Friday — I set aside fifteen - thirty minutes on each day to do my personal and business finances.
- Website Wednesday - I do not enjoy working on my website, so I make sure I schedule time in on Wednesday to do little tasks on my website.
- Fridge Friday - Another task I dread, so I set time aside on Fridays to clean out my refrigerator.
- Supper Saturday or Sunday — Take some time to meal plan for the week.

Create your own!

3. Create a Self-care Journal

There is a blank journal page for you to use at the end of this chapter and also a sample of my client's journal. Use this journal to plan which self-care actions you will take each day. These are rituals that you enjoy doing and also actions you resist doing. Remember you are the manager of your life, and you know what works best for you. You can make several copies, bind them in a three-ring folder or binder and decorate the front if you wish and make it uniquely yours. Fill in the date and the things you do each day. There is a place for morning rituals and evening rituals. In this place you can fill in the self-care rituals that work best for you.

4. Get Moving

Exercise is also a unique activity for all. Do what works best for you and find movement or exercise that you like to do. Carve out at least thirty minutes four times a week. When I am busy working on a project, I try to get up at least every thirty minutes and move. Sometimes I dance to music, sometimes I do twenty reps up and down my steps. When I write or paint, I always have to make sure I get up and move to keep the ideas flowing. Some of my favorite exercise videos are by Erin Stutland, who has these quick five-minute workouts if you don't have a lot of time. She has longer sessions available, too. Erin also has these Soul Strolls that you can listen to while you walk that are fabulous. They are thirty-minute music soundtracks infused with mantras to help you take action in your life. I take a walk almost every day because walking feeds my creative spirit.

5. Get Laughing

Ahh, laughter, one of my favorite things to do! Make it a point to add laughter to your life. Who doesn't like a good laugh? A good belly laugh is great for your health and your abs. Laughter is contagious, especially the kind when you start and just can't seem to stop yourself no matter what. This has happened to me on more than one occasion; you know, when you are in that place where you shouldn't be laughing, like school or church. I remember one time when I was young, my cousin and I got separated in church by the usher for laughing in church. The separation didn't solve the problem though; we could still see each other from our different pews, and we continued to laugh. I love this story; it still makes me laugh today. I am laughing as I write this and I hope you feel this energy. I have a whole list of funny stories filed away in my memory and I share them often. My childhood friends always tell me what a great memory I have; we love to reminisce and share our amusing stories. Think of a funny story from the past and laugh and share it with the person who helped you create that funny memory. Seek out comical jokes, watch a funny movie, don't take life so seriously, laugh a little each day.

6. Stop Saying Yes When You Mean No

This is easier said than done. Some of us have such deep people-pleasing programming that it is hard for us to say no. We just keep saying yes and then, in the end, no one including ourselves, our kids or our spouse, benefits. Sometimes we need to elicit the help of a friend or a health or life coach with this one to help keep us accountable.

7. Look Into Self-development Tools that Can Help You Further Understand Yourself

An example could be Numerology, Astrology, Human Design and the Meyers Briggs test.

8. Don't Participate in the Comparing Game

Refraining from the comparing game is way easier said than done because since we were born, we have been continuously compared to others, whether it be in school, work or with peers. Learn how to become aware when you are comparing, which is most likely several times a day. You can use this awareness to either refrain from comparing (which is hard to do), or if you have already started the harsh comparisons in your mind, you can reframe them. Ask yourself, what is it that I would like to bring into my life? Maybe share the comparison with your release buddy so you can release it and figure out what you want to bring into your life. If you are comparing yourself to someone who is thin, maybe you want to lose weight or eat healthier. Use the awareness of the energy of comparison to help you take action to bring something you desire into your life.

Remember that the people we are comparing ourselves to are human too. They have human emotions and struggles just like us. They have tribulations and triumphs in their life just like us. Stay in your lane and take actions that only you can take.

"Since you are like no other being ever created since the beginning of time, you are incomparable."

- Brenda Ueland

Recipes and Rituals for Self-care

Oil Pulling

I have been oil pulling every day for a little over five years. I use coconut oil. There are so many benefits that come from oil pulling. The most significant thing I noticed is it keeps me from getting stomach bugs and other viruses that are going around.

What do you need?

1 t coconut oil or another oil such as sesame

How to do it:

1. Do it first thing in the morning upon waking. You don't want to drink any water or brush your teeth because you are removing the germs that grew overnight.

2. Place a teaspoon of coconut oil in your mouth and swish.

Some sources say that you have to do this for at least twenty minutes a day to receive maximum benefits. I find that sometimes I can do this and other times I can't. Listen to your body. I still feel like I gain the benefits even when I don't do it for twenty minutes. Spit oil in the trash can and then rinse your mouth with warm water and brush your teeth.

Benefits:

- Helps with dental hygiene
- Whitens teeth
- Boosts your immune system
- Increases energy
- Helps clear your skin

Dry Brushing

This is another ritual that I have been doing for over five years. I keep the dry brush by the shower and quickly do it before I jump in. I don't do it every day, just a few times a week. I know, I know you might say you don't have time and that you are in a rush. But it only takes five minutes and is well worth it.

What do you need?

A natural bristle brush with a long handle and five minutes.

How to do it:

1. Start at your feet and always brush in a circular motion towards your heart.
2. Start with your feet and work your way up.
3. Apply less pressure in sensitive areas.
4. Take a shower or a bath when finished.

Benefits:

- Stimulates your lymphatic system and can aid in getting rid of toxins and waste in your body
- It can help reduce cellulite
- Removes dead skin
- Improves circulation
- Gives you an energy boost

Epsom Salt Baths

Epsom salt baths are another ritual that is a must on my list. I look forward to this ritual and feel a difference when I am done.

What do you need?

1 cup Epsom salt
½ cup baking soda
A few drops of essential oils

How to do it :

1. Fill the tub with warm water and add the Epsom salt, baking soda, and essential oils I like to alternate — sometimes I add sea salt.
2. Soak for at least 20 minutes.
3. Gently towel dry your body and moisturize your body with a chemical-free moisturizer, or you can use an oil such as coconut or sesame.

Benefits:

- Reduces stress and relaxes you
- Boosts magnesium levels
- Flushes toxins from your body
- Reduces inflammation in the body

Epsom Salt Scrubs

If you don't have access to a tub or don't like baths, you can make an Epsom salt scrub for the shower and enjoy the same benefits as an Epsom salt bath.

What do you need?

1 cup Epsom salt
½ cup coconut oil or almond oil
1 T Vitamin E oil
10 drops of essential oil of your choice

How to do it:

1. Mix all the ingredients in a bowl.
2. Transfer to an airtight jar.

I like to use a mix of rosemary and eucalyptus for my morning shower because these essential oils invigorate you, clear fatigue and stimulate the brain, and lavender if I am taking a shower at night because it is calming.

Lavender Lime DIY Deodorant

It is no secret that the ingredients in deodorant we buy and use have many harmful ingredients that can interfere with our health. That is why I started making my own deodorant. Many of the recipes call for baking soda. However, the baking soda irritated my skin, so I created this recipe.

What do you need?

¼ cup arrowroot
¼ cup organic cornstarch
½ cup coconut oil
15 drops of lavender essential oil
10 drops of lime essential oil

How to do it:

1. Mix dry ingredients in a bowl.
2. Add in coconut oil and mash with a fork.
3. Add the oils.
4. Transfer to an airtight jar.
5. Rub a bit under your arm after your shower or as needed.

Benefits:

- You are not putting harmful chemicals on your skin.
- This recipe lasts a while so you can save money.

Honey Face Mask

I love honey and use it for many different healthy purposes. For example, it contains antioxidants, it is anti-bacterial and anti-fungal, aids with sleep, helps with seasonal allergies and is a natural cough syrup.

It is perfect for skin. I try to do a honey mask weekly when I take a bath.

Make sure you purchase raw local honey or Manuka honey

What do you need?

2 T raw or Manuka honey
3 drops of lavender essential oil

How to do it:

1. Mix the 2 ingredients in a glass bowl or jar.
2. Clean your face with a natural cleanser.
3. Apply the mask to the face and let sit for 15 minutes.
4. Use a warm cloth to wipe off the honey mask.

Benefits:

*   There is an antibacterial agent in honey, so it is great for acne prevention and treatment
*   It helps with aging because honey is full of antioxidants.
*   Moisturizes skin and gives you a glow.

Chocolate Sugar Scrub

I love this pampering self-care recipe. When I use it, I feel like I am at a spa. Around the holidays, you can whip some up for gifts and decorate the jars.

What do you need?

½ cup raw cane sugar
½ cup organic brown sugar
½ cup coconut oil, almond oil or olive oil
2 T organic cacao powder
A few drops of pure vanilla extract

How to do it:

1. Mix the dry ingredients in a bowl.
2. Then add the oil and vanilla and mix.
3. Transfer to an airtight jar.

Benefits:

*   Hydrates the skin.
*   Gently exfoliates the skin.

Daily Journal

Date _____

"Well done is better than well said."

- Ben Franklin

Morning Rituals: _____

_____

_____

_____

The one thing I don't want to do today. Get it out of the way so you can enjoy your day! _____

_____

_____

_____

Other things to do today - Don't overload yourself; remember you are human.

_____

_____

_____

_____

Evening Rituals: _____

_____

_____

_____

Gratitude and Appreciation:_____

_____

_____

_____

Reflect on your day. Take a few minutes to think about your day. What were your triumphs? Your tribulations? Is there anything you would do differently? Do not beat yourself up over your tribulations. Reflecting on them is meant for you to see that you are a work in progress and tomorrow is a new day and new beginning.

_____

_____

_____

_____

Go to bed with a happy thought!

Client's Sample Daily Journal

"Well done is better than well said."

- Ben Franklin

Morning Rituals:

Oil pull

Pray/Inspired Action

Take a walk with the family

The one thing I don't want to do today. Get it out of the way so you can enjoy your day! Write out bills

Other things to do today - Don't overload yourself; remember you are human.

Paint

Make cookies for school function

Make healthy meal for family/meal prep for week

Evening Rituals

Take Epsom salt bath

Relax and journal in front of the fire

Evening Rituals:

Take Epsom salt bath

Relax and journal in front of the fire

Gratitude and Appreciation:

I am grateful for the sunny day and a walk with my family.

I am grateful for the painting I created today that I hope to sell at my art show.

I am grateful for the work I am doing with my health coach.

I am grateful that I am eating healthy and not putting too much on my plate.

I am grateful that I am learning to say no to things that overwhelm me.

Reflect on your day. Take a few minutes to think about your day. What were your triumphs? Your tribulations? Is there anything you would do differently? Do not beat yourself up over your tribulations. Reflecting on them is meant for you to see that you are a work in progress and tomorrow is a new day and new beginning.

It is sometimes hard for me to say no, because I feel bad. But I am having better days because I am learning to do this. I am happy I am getting to this place. It feels like a triumph. This section used to be filled with tribulations. I didn't get a chance to journal and relax by the fire but I think I put too many things on my list again.

Go to bed with a happy thought!

See everything you do as a moment of opening up to the creativity of the universe. Don't judge any moment or task as dull or unfulfilling. Instead, use each moment to be fully alive — find the joy in everyday living.

The shadow voice and social programming make us believe that some moments aren't good enough and we will be happier when we get here or there.

Everything is created in the present moment. So, create your life one moment at a time.

#6

TREAT YOUR BODY LIKE A WORK OF ART

Sunflowers

"Our bodies are God's art; treat them like His masterpiece."

- Christine Burke

The July sun gleamed through my bedroom window as I got dressed in my white cut-off shorts and yellow sun top that tied at the shoulders. I looked at myself in the mirror and smiled. I was one of those kids who loved clothes. I liked the texture and loved modeling my outfits.

My dad yelled up to me, "Hurry up, it is time to leave."

"I'll be right down," I said loudly as I finished off my outfit with a yellow headband. I looked in the mirror one more time and then skipped out of my bedroom, excited for our family day.

I jumped in the backseat of my family's maroon Chevy. We were headed to our weekly Saturday lunch at my grandparents' house. Cold cuts, Italian rolls, potato chips and tasty cakes were always served, a real treat for my brother, sisters and me, especially since our mom was a health nut and these foods were rarely, if ever, served at our house.

We pulled up to their house in the city, a red brick raised ranch. I leaped out of the car. As I climbed the steps to their house, I looked down at my legs and my white cut-off shorts and admired my outfit once more. I felt good!

But something changed that day ...

After lunch, we went into my grandparents' backyard to play badminton, another Saturday tradition. I felt my grandfather staring at my legs. He was a thin Italian man with looks that always caught people's attention. He rarely had a nice word to say, but he showed love by giving us money each time we saw him and surprising us with gifts or vacations. His dad died when he was just four and a half years old, and his mother enrolled him in a boarding school for fatherless boys. He attended this school for twelve years and from his stories I sensed it was a cold, lonely upbringing which brought about his rigid and

> *authoritarian way.*
>
> *After I served, he called me aside and asked, "How much did you eat? Look at your legs; they are getting fat. You shouldn't eat so much; you need to start watching what you eat." I felt a knot in my stomach and no longer felt like playing badminton. I wanted to run and hide in a closet.*

After that day in my grandfather's backyard, he started weighing me when I went to his house. I shuddered in fear as I looked at the scale, hoping it didn't say more than the last time I was on it.

I was around twelve years old when this story happened. On that day, a war inside me started with my body and food. It lasted a very long time.

Many of us have a story like this, a time when we were stripped of an innocent appreciation and freedom towards our bodies.

This one incident led me on a lifelong battle of trying every diet there was — counting points, counting calories, cleanses, soup diets, not eating after 6 pm, the 80/20 rule (which I found to be the only gem in the bunch).

You name it, and I tried it!

It seemed the more diets I tried, the more frustrated I became. I deprived myself and went to be bed starving so many nights.

Until I came to heal these stories that were controlling me.

Coincidentally, I started healing these stories when I started using my emotions to create. Like I shared earlier, I took my feelings and turned them into words and paintings that helped me let go of the stories that were ruling me. Creativity allowed me to heal this place inside of me and helped me see the beauty in all things and all people. I began to feel compassion towards my grandfather and his upbringing. I saw that he did the best he could, given his circumstances. Slowly, I was able to turn my wounds into wisdom. I began to talk to my grandfather in Heaven, and I now see him as my guardian angel. I feel his love and support. He has given me so many signs that he is around me. I hear songs we listened to when I ask for help, and he has sent signs from people. Over the years I have met people that went to the same boarding school as him. There really are no coincidences when you open up to the world of spirit.

Through art, I was able to see my body as a gift from God; I was able to see my body with all its imperfections as God's art. Like a painting, I saw myself as a work in progress — an unfinished masterpiece that was still being touched up and developed. This helped me deal with my so-called imperfections and the imperfections of others. I started to be grateful for my body.

Don't Starve Yourself

From my experience and in working with clients, I have found the best way to live is not to starve yourself but to eat healthy whole foods when you are hungry. We are more in the creative flow of life when we are not obsessed with rules like don't eat after six pm or eat this and don't eat that.

I remember hearing a quote from Geneen Roth - "For every diet, there's an equal and opposite binge."

Diets restrict us and don't take into consideration the needs of the individual.

It seems that when someone gives us a rule around diet and exercise, or just hands us a list of foods to eat, or an exercise plan, at some point there will be something in us that wants to rebel and go to the opposite extreme. I find that whenever I am too strict with anything in life, whether it be a diet or a schedule, at some point I want to do the direct opposite. So, it is best to live life in that middle place where we learn to live our best selves. We sit in the middle of the see-saw able to see starving is the same as binging. Enjoying life in the middle grounds us and then we can use food to fuel our bodies.

New books, diets and ideas for weight loss are always coming out saying eat this but don't eat that. This can make our heads spin and we use all our energy chasing that next diet, only to be left feeling confused, frustrated and drained of life force.

What if we listened to our intuition and bodies and decided what worked best for us?

What if we listened and treated ourselves and our bodies with respect?

What I am going to offer you in this chapter are guidelines for eating healthy, so you have the sustained energy to go after those creative dreams of yours. These are not rules, simply guidelines to follow; the most important thing is that you get quiet and listen to your body to see what is best for you.

There is also a list of foods that can help you plan and decide what to eat for breakfast, lunch and dinner, followed by some of my favorite recipes for each meal. I left room for you to be creative so that you can add your unique flair to the recipes and your life.

Like the other chapters, there are also activities. These activities are designed to help you come up with a way of living and nourishing the inner artist that is right for you.

Due to my allergy, I maintain a gluten-free and dairy-free diet. I fill my plate with lots of whole foods like fruits and vegetables. I do eat a little bit of meat and grain. A lot of the recipes have rice and pasta options because I am feeding a growing teenage boy.

I have learned not to put too much on my plate both literally and physically. These restrictions aren't right for everyone, and I would never want to push this way of living on anyone. This may seem strict for some and it may not meet your needs. So I invite you to listen, experiment and come up with a plan that is best for you. Take charge of your plate and fill it with things that nourish your mind, body and soul.

The Well-Nourished Artist Guidelines

- Eat healthy whole foods. Try to stay away from processed foods and refined sugar and limit your alcohol intake.

- Don't think about diet or restriction; think about adding healthy whole foods to your diet.

- Use Inspired Action Meditation to help you listen to your body and intuition and come up with what works best for you.

- Love your body and find ways to appreciate it.

- Apply the 80/20 rule to eating. I have found the 80/20 rule to be very beneficial over the years. This consists of eating a healthy diet 80% of the time and eating "treats" the other 20%. For example, I eat a gluten-free, dairy-free diet with little or no processed foods. So, for my 20% of the time, I still stick to having no gluten or dairy, and my 20% includes having French fries or homemade sweet treats. I have some sweet treat recipes at the end of this chapter.

- Slow down when you are eating, take the time to say a small prayer of appreciation before you eat and chew your food slowly. Taking the time to chew your food is great for digestion and gut health.

- Drink water.

- If you do a cleanse, do it with a healthy mindset, not a restrictive one.

Activities

1. Meal Planning and Prep

I mentioned in the previous chapter how I carve out some time on Saturday or Sunday to meal plan and prep. At the end of this chapter is a sheet I use to guide me with my weekly meal planning. There is a blank one for you to reproduce and also two sample meal plans. I make staples on Sunday or Monday that I can add to meals during the week, for example, brown rice, hard-boiled eggs, quinoa, prepared salads and snacks or treats. I also like to cook two meals in one night. For example, if I am making salmon cakes one night, I cook some extra salmon to make sushi the following night. There are so many benefits to meal planning, such as it can inspire you to eat healthier, save you money, spark your creativity in the kitchen and help you remain calm during the week because you aren't stressing about what you should eat.

2. Meditate

You can use the meditation from the "Creativity Thieves" chapter to help you discover stories around your body that may have given you a negative mindset towards it. Create a ritual around releasing these stories and rewrite the story.

3. Listen to Your Intuition and Body

Now that you are in tune with your intuition and body through Inspired Action Meditation pay attention to the foods that make you feel good and give you energy. Be aware of the foods you might be eating that are not making you feel well. This activity isn't about being strict on yourself, but about listening to your body.

4. Crowd Out Unhealthy Food with Healthy Foods

The Institute of Integrative Nutrition coined a concept called 'Crowding Out'. This concept focuses on adding more fruit, vegetables and foods that are rich in nutrients to your diet. This naturally crowds out the foods that aren't good for you because you don't have room. This concept can take some time but stick with it and you will find it can be more effective than fad diets. When working with this concept with my clients I encourage them to try a new healthy food every week, such as a vegetable, herb or fruit they haven't tried before.

5. Consult with a Doctor to See which Vitamins/Supplements Might be Right for You

The 4 most popular that are recommended by most health gurus are a good multivitamin, vitamin D3, a probiotic, and a fish oil. Of course, there are other vitamins that might be recommended and you can also receive many vitamins from your foods. Look for vitamins that are non-GMO and don't have any fillers. When I am meal prepping, I also prep my vitamins in a weekly vitamin container.

Also, add the most important supplement of all to your life and your recipes - Vitamin L

When you are meal planning or cooking, invite the energy of love in and add it to your meals. It is so easy to do and it shifts your vibration.

My daughter's friends heard me mention it one time they were over, and now it is a running joke, they will say, "Mrs. Burke, I can tell you added Vitamin L to these cookies." One time I was cooking and not in the best mood and my son called me on it. He said jokingly, "Hmmm, doesn't look like you are adding the Vitamin L today." It gave me a chuckle and helped me shift my energy and I was able to add love to the recipe.

6. Get Fancy with Your Water

Add different fruits, veggies and herbs to your water to make it more appealing. Creating different water recipes each week makes me feel like I am at a spa. I like to serve them in fancy glasses. My favorite water to make in the summer is watermelon, lime and mint. Another good tip is to get yourself a nice water bottle and always fill it ahead of time. I have found filling the bottle first thing in the morning or the night before if you have to rush out the door early, helps you stick with drinking all your water.

7. Work With a Health Coach to Help Guide You and Hold You Accountable.

8. Use the Integrative Nutrition® Plate

The Institute for Integrative Nutrition® (IIN®) teaches a number of dietary theories and concepts. The Integrative Nutrition® Plate, pictured below, conveys nutritional and lifestyle guidelines for optimal health and wellbeing. Unlike most government diagrams, which focus primarily on food, the Integrative Nutrition® Plate incorporates Relationships, Spirituality, Career, and Physical Activity as four additional areas we must nourish in order to thrive.

The Institute for Integrative Nutrition® (IIN®) founder, Joshua Rosenthal, coined the terms Primary Food and Secondary Food. Primary Food refers to everything that feeds us that is not food. Primary Food such as our careers, relationships, spirituality, physical activity, finances, education, environment, social life, and other lifestyle factors play an equal if not more significant role in the quality of our lives than what is on our plates.

In contrast, Secondary Food is the actual food we eat: fruits, vegetables, grains, proteins, and fats. Secondary Food does not provide the fulfilment Primary Food provides, but oftentimes we use it to suppress our hunger for Primary Food.

Remember, people need more than their nutritional needs met in order to be healthy; they need love, movement, stability, adventure, purpose and creativity in order to thrive.

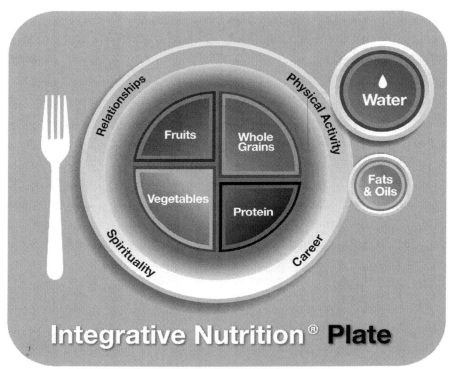

Integrative Nutrition® Plate

9. Refer to the Clean Fifteen List and Dirty Dozen to Help You Decide When to Buy Organic

I like to purchase mostly organic ingredients; however, this can get very costly. Each year, the Environmental Working Group puts out a Clean Fifteen and Dirty Dozen List. They research fruits and vegetables that contain the most pesticides. You can keep this list in mind when purchasing your produce to help you decide which fruits and vegetables to buy organic. Below is the list from 2017:

2017 Dirty Dozen List

1. Strawberries
2. Spinach
3. Nectarines
4. Apples
5. Peaches
6. Pears
7. Cherries
8. Grapes
9. Celery
10. Tomatoes
11. Sweet bell peppers
12. Potatoes

2017 Clean Fifteen List

1. Sweet corn
2. Avocados
3. Pineapple
4. Cabbage
5. Onions
6. Frozen sweet peas
7. Papayas
8. Asparagus
9. Mangoes
10. Eggplant
11. Honeydew melon
12. Kiwi
13. Cantaloupe
14. Cauliflower
15. Grapefruit

Sample Ideas/List of Things to Eat for Breakfast, Lunch, Dinner, and Snacking

Below is a sample of different items you can eat for meals and snacks – it is broken into categories. This list is useful in helping you with meal planning and creating meals that work for you. After the food list is a sampling of recipes from each category.

Cooking wasn't always one of my favorite things to do but, let's face it, it is something we usually have to do unless we have a personal chef. Years ago, I would often resent cooking because I felt like my time was better spent painting or writing. Inviting the creative part of me into the kitchen (and all areas of my life) has shifted the way I look at things and has made cooking and life so much more fun. Creativity doesn't stop when you put away your paints or pen or put down your guitar. It is a beautiful spirit and a muse that we invite into every aspect of our lives.

Breakfast
Oatmeal
Sweet potato toast with nut butter
Fruit
Hardboiled eggs
Flaxseed muffin
Chia oatmeal jars
Granola with unsweetened coconut yogurt
Smoothies
Egg muffins
Protein/Paleo pancakes
Quinoa breakfast bake

Lunch
Salads
Portion of leftovers from the night before
Soups

Dinner
Soup and a salad
Stir fry
Salmon cake and veggies
Brown rice pasta with veggies and chicken
Tacos, beans and guacamole
Honey lime chicken and spicy sweet potato fries
Veggie fried rice
Homemade sushi
Chili
Soups

Snacks
Hummus and veggies
Guacamole with veggies
Fruit
Popcorn - fresh popped
Chili lime cashews
Trail mixes
Nuts

Drinks
Smoothies
Kombucha
Water with fruit, veggies and herbs
Turmeric tonic

Sweet Treats
Oatmeal cookies
Granola
Cashew butter balls
Energy balls
Chocolate coconut candy or bark
Iced cashew coffee
Hot chocolate with whipped cream

Recipes for The Well-Nourished Artist

Breakfast

We all know the importance of eating breakfast - your body needs fuel after the fast. It is essential to eat a meal that is high in nutrition in the morning. Eating a healthy breakfast can improve your concentration, give you strength and get your day off to a good start. I have a ritual where I always say a small prayer of gratitude before eating my breakfast.

One-minute FlaxSeed Muffin - Inspired by Genius Kitchen

Serves 1

These are my favorite and a staple in my house. A nice warm muffin for breakfast on a cold morning brings me joy! I love thinking of new fruits and nuts I can add to them.

Ingredients

¼ cup flaxseed meal
½ t baking soda
¼ t stevia, honey or other sweeter
1 t cinnamon
1 egg
1 t oil (I use coconut oil)

Optional - berries, nuts, unsweetened cherries, vegan chocolate chips, nuts, etc.

A pinch of Vitamin L❤

Directions

1. If adding the optional items to the muffin, mix them with a little gluten-free flour and add to rest of mixture; the flour will help them stay in place and not sink to the bottom of the muffin.

2. Mix all the dry ingredients in a mug and then add egg, oil and liquid sweeter. Put in the microwave for one minute. If you use berries, it will be very moist at first, but it dries as it cools.

Breakfast Egg Muffins

Serves 6

These are great to make on the weekend and have some for breakfast during the week. You can store them in the refrigerator or freeze them. You can also get creative and experiment with other ingredients such as olives, onions, kale, etc.

Ingredients

10 eggs
½ cup spinach, chopped
1 red pepper, chopped
1/3 cup of cooked meat — bacon/sausage (optional)
Non-stick cooking spray or coconut oil
Salt and pepper to taste
Garnish with Vitamin L♥

Directions

1. Preheat oven to 375 degrees.
2. Spray the muffin pan with cooking spray or use coconut oil (I like to use coconut oil because I love the flavor).
3. In a large cooking bowl, whisk the eggs and then add other ingredients and mix.
4. Pour the mixture into the muffin pans about 3/4 of the way.
5. Bake for 15-20 minutes.
6. Enjoy them hot or store in refrigerator for future meals.

Quinoa Breakfast Bake - Inspired by Pop Sugar

Serves 6

This is so delicious, especially hot out of the oven but it certainly tastes great reheated or cold. A great go-to breakfast treat. In the summer I like to replace the apples with fresh peaches or sometimes I use frozen peaches. You can also experiment with other fruits and spices, for example, blueberry with lemon zest.

Ingredients

1 cup uncooked quinoa
3 apples peeled and diced
2 eggs
2 cups vanilla coconut milk (or other milk)
¼ maple syrup
1 ½ t cinnamon
¼ t nutmeg
A sprinkle ground cloves
Non-stick cooking spray or coconut oil
A touch of sea salt
Drizzle with Vitamin L ❤

Directions

1. Preheat oven to 350 degrees.

2. Grease an 8x8 baking dish with coconut oil.

3. In a small bowl mix the uncooked quinoa with all the spices and the sea salt.

4. Pour it into the greased baking dish.

5. Sprinkle the apples on top.

6. In the small bowl, beat the eggs then add the milk and maple syrup and whisk.

7. Pour the mixture over the top of the apples and quinoa and stir lightly.

8. Bake for 1 hour.

9. Allow to cool and then cut into squares. Store leftovers in refrigerator, reheat and serve.

Chia Oatmeal in a Jar

These are the best. You can make the jars ahead of time. I usually make three at a time and keep the jars in the refrigerator. It makes me so happy when I am on the go and have a wholesome breakfast to enjoy. These are great to do seasonally. Eating seasonally has many benefits, such as it tastes better, is cost effective and the produce has a higher nutritional value since it is fresher.

Here are 4 of my favorite recipes.

Peach and Pecan Perfection

Serves 1

Ingredients

3 T gluten-free oats
2 T chia seeds
2 T pecans
1 t maple syrup or your favorite sweetener
½ t cinnamon
½ fresh peaches (or thawed frozen peaches)
1 cup coconut milk (or almond, cashew, etc.)
A pinch of Vitamin L ❤

Directions

1. Place the dry ingredients in the jar and mix.
2. Then add milk and peaches and stir again.
3. Place in the refrigerator overnight.

Chocolate Banana Dream

Serves 1

Ingredients

3 T gluten-free oats
2 T chia seeds
2 T walnuts
1 T cocoa powder
A splash of vanilla
½ banana sliced
1 cup coconut milk (or almond, cashew, etc.)
A pinch of Vitamin L ❤

Directions

1. Place the dry ingredients in the jar and mix.

2. Then add milk and bananas and stir again.

3. Place in the refrigerator overnight.

Summer Berries

Serves 1

Ingredients

3 T gluten-free oats
2 T chia seeds
2 t flaxseed meal
¼ cup seasonal berries (blackberries, strawberries or blueberries)
A splash of vanilla
1 cup coconut milk (or almond, cashew, etc.)
A pinch of Vitamin L ❤

Directions

1. Place the dry ingredients in the jar and mix.

2. Then add milk and berries and stir again.

3. Place in the refrigerator overnight.

Pumpkin Spice Delight

Serves 1

Ingredients

3 T gluten-free oats
2 T chia seeds
2 T pumpkin seeds
½ t cinnamon
¼ t nutmeg
A sprinkle of ginger
1 t maple syrup
1/3 cup pumpkin puree
1 cup coconut milk (or almond, cashew, etc.)
A pinch of Vitamin L ❤

Directions

1. Place the dry ingredients in the jar and mix.

2. Then add milk and berries and stir again.

3. Place in the refrigerator overnight.

Smoothies

Smoothies are all the rage these days and for a good reason. You can pack a bunch of nutrients into just one drink. Smoothies are a great breakfast addition, especially if you are someone who doesn't like to eat in the morning.

Smoothies can be made fresh in the morning or you can prep them ahead of time. Place all the dry ingredients and fruit/veggies in a jar and store in the refrigerator, then in the morning you can add the liquid.

I usually pick two smoothie recipes for the week: this way you don't have buy too many ingredients.

Smoothies can also be enjoyed throughout the day. Here are a few of my favorite smoothie recipes. After the recipes are a list of smoothie items you can pick and choose from. This list will help you get creative and whip up your unique smoothie recipes.

Salted Chocolate Smoothie

Serves 1

Ingredients

1 ¼ cup milk (coconut or almond)
2 T chia seeds
2 T cacao powder or cacao nibs
1 t Maca powder (optional)
1 t nut butter (I like cashew butter)
1 t coconut oil (if you haven't used coconut oil before, start with just a little bit and gradually build up to a teaspoon)
A handful of spinach
1 t organic maple syrup, honey or stevia to sweeten or fruit like half of a banana
Ice
Sea salt to taste
A spoonful of Vitamin L ❤

Directions

1.   Place all ingredients in a high-speed blender and blend until smooth.

You can get creative and try different things, for example, a 1/2 of banana, strawberries to sweeten, add flaxseed, hemp seeds or goji berries.

Tropical Summer Smoothie

Serves 1

Ingredients

½ cup unsweetened coconut water
½ cup filtered water
¾ cup greens — spinach, kale or watercress
½ cucumber
1 t coconut oil
1 T chia seeds
½ cup frozen pineapple; if you use fresh add ice cubes
Juice of 1 lime
A pinch of ginger
A few kiwi slices (optional)
Ice
Sprinkle with Vitamin L ❤

Directions

1. Place all the ingredients into a high-speed blender and blend until smooth.

Berry Good Smoothie

Serves 1

Ingredients

1 cup frozen berries
Juice of ½ orange
Juice of 1 lime
½ cup unsweetened coconut water
½ cup water
Ice
Add Vitamin L as needed ❤

Directions

1. Place all the ingredients into a high-speed blender and blend until smooth.

Green Love

Serves 1

Ingredients

Large handful parsley
Small handful cilantro
Cucumber, peeled and chopped
½ cup blueberries
Juice of 1 lemon
Juice of 1 lime
Juice of ½ orange
Water
Ice
Lots of Vitamin L ❤

Directions

1. Place all ingredients in a high-speed blender and blend until smooth.

Basil Detox Smoothie

Serves 1

Ingredients

5-6 leaves of fresh basil
Large handful of fresh spinach
1 green apple peeled and chopped
Juice of 2 lemons
Small piece of ginger
1 t coconut oil
Ice
A pinch of Vitamin L ❤

Directions

1. Place all ingredients into a high-speed blender and blend until smooth.

Turmeric Tonic Smoothie

Serves 1

Ingredients

1 T ginger peeled
2 T fresh numeric grated
1 apple peeled and chopped
Juice of ½ orange
Juice of 2 lemons
1 cup water or unsweetened coconut water
Pinch of black pepper
Ice (optional)
A dose of Vitamin L ❤

Directions

1. Place all ingredients in a high-speed blender and blend until smooth.

* I often make a bigger batch of this drink and do not add ice. Store it in the refrigerator in an airtight container.

A Variety of Ingredients to Use for Smoothie Recipes

Pick one or two items from each list and create your own smoothie recipe.

Veggies
Spinach
Kale
Watercress
Cucumbers
Basil
Carrots
Celery
Beets
Bok choy
Dandelion greens
Fruits
Blueberries
Strawberries
Raspberries
Cherries
Lemon
Lime
Orange
Avocado
Pineapple
Mango
Banana
Kiwi

* Anytime your fresh fruit is starting to get old, throw it in the freezer and use it in your smoothies so you don't waste it. When you use frozen fruit in your smoothies you usually don't have to add ice.

Superfoods
Cacao powder
Chia seeds
Chlorella
Maca powder
Wheatgrass

Hemp seeds
Nuts or Nut Butters
Cashew
Almond
Peanuts

Herbs and Spices
Ginger
Cinnamon
Mint
Turmeric and black pepper
Parsley
Cloves
Vanilla
Milk
Coconut
Almond
Cashew
Oils
Coconut
Avocado
Macadamia

Lunch

I think salads are the best go-to for lunches. Like smoothies, salads are another opportunity to call in your creativity. I already shared that I started eating salads before the age of two and I started creating them shortly after. Coincidently, as I was gathering recipes for salads, a friend mine texted me and said, "Do you remember when we were at the retreat in Florida and the restaurant named a salad after you?" I took a look at all the salads on the menu and asked the waiter if I could create my own and next thing you know everybody was ordering 'The Christine Salad'. I find a key to life is mixing things up, so try to add variety to your salads so you don't get bored with the same old salads; add fruit, nuts and experiment. Below are a few salad recipes.

Chick Pea Salad

Serves 4

This is a great one to make on Sunday or Monday and then eat for lunch for a few days. It usually is good for up to 3 days in the refrigerator. If you are making it ahead of time, you can store the dressing in an airtight container and add it as you eat. You can also add the avocado on the day you are eating it, so you don't have to worry about it getting too soft. I love to eat this salad over a bed of lettuce.

Ingredients

1 15 oz. can chick peas
2 avocados, diced
1 cucumber, medium to large dices
1 red onion, chopped
2 cups grape tomatoes, halved
Juice of 1 lime
6 - 8 leaves of basil, chopped
Salt and pepper to taste
Drizzle with Vitamin L ❤

Directions

1. Mix together avocado, cucumber, onion and tomatoes.
2. Add the juice of lime.
3. Add basil and salt and pepper and toss.

Dressing

Ingredients

½ cup olive oil
¼ cup red wine vinegar
6-8 leaves of basil, chopped
Salt and pepper to taste

Directions

1. Place all ingredients in a blender and blend until smooth

Brown Rice Salad

Serves 4

This is also another great salad to prep ahead of time and enjoy for a few days. To add variety to this, sprinkle cashews or almonds on it, add chicken, black olives or try using a different kind of bean. I sometimes use quinoa instead of brown rice. This is another great salad to enjoy over a bed of lettuce.

Ingredients

2 cups cooked brown rice
1 15 oz. can pinto beans
1 cucumber, peeled and chopped
2 cups grape tomatoes, halved
A few sprigs of cilantro, chopped
3-4 scallions, sliced
Drizzle with Vitamin L ❤

Directions

1. In large bowl add rice and all other ingredients then mix.

2. Chill before serving

Dressing

Ingredients

½ cup olive oil
2 T Braggs organic coconut liquid aminos (a good alternative for soy sauce)
Juice of ½ lime
1 t honey
1/8 t cumin
Salt and pepper to taste

Directions

1. Add all ingredients to blender and blend until smooth.

2. Pour dressing over salad.

Colorful Salad

What can I say? I love color and this salad always brightens my day. If you want you can wash and cut all ingredients and then store them in separate containers to create the salad each time or toss it in a bowl and serve it to the family.

Ingredients

1 large clamshell of Spring mix or lettuce of your choice
1 small head of purple cabbage
1 red onion, sliced
2 cups grape 2 tomatoes, halved
2 carrots, shredded
1 yellow pepper, sliced
½ cup radishes, sliced
1 medium beet, sliced
¾ cup almond slivers
Garnish with Vitamin L ❤

Directions

1. Wash and cut all ingredients.

2. Toss in a large bowl.

3. Serve with homemade dressing.

Dinner

Dinner seems to be the hardest meal to plan. Below are quick and easy recipes I have created over the years. They are gluten-free and dairy-free recipes, but you can adjust them to fit your dietary needs for example, substitute the grain or pasta for regular and also any of the coconut milk for other milks.

Salmon Cakes

Serves 4

These are great to eat as leftovers the next day for lunch. I like to put one on top of a salad. Usually when I make these, I make extra and freeze them.

Ingredients

1 lb. cooked salmon
¼ cup onion, minced
½ cup almond flour
2 eggs
Juice of ½ lemon
2 T mayonnaise (homemade)
1 t Dijon mustard
2 sprigs dill, chopped
Salt and pepper to taste
Vitamin L to taste ❤

Directions

1. Beat eggs and mix in mayo, mustard and mix in lemon juice.
2. Add onion, fish, almond flour and fold.
3. Add dill, salt and pepper.
4. Chill mix for at least 30 minutes.
5. Shape into patties.
6. Preheat oven to 375.
7. Sauté in coconut oil for a few minutes on each side until brown.
8. Finish off by baking in oven for 10 minutes.

Pasta and Veggies in a Cream Sauce

Serves 4

This is a creamy and delicious meal and you can add whatever protein you like to this dish - chicken, shrimp, tofu, etc.

Ingredients

3 T olive oil or coconut oil
2 T garlic minced
2 cups grape tomatoes, halved
3 T fresh basil, chopped
4 cups fresh baby spinach
¾ cup coconut milk
Cooked Pasta of choice - brown rice, bean, zucchini or quinoa pasta
Protein Optional - shrimp, chicken, etc.
Garnish with Vitamin L ❤

Directions

1. Heat the oil in a large pan, add garlic and sauté for 2 minutes.

2. Add the tomatoes and heat another minute.

3. Next add the basil and cooked protein if you choose.

4. Toss in the spinach and then add coconut milk to heat, and you can also drizzle with a little more olive oil.

5. Serve over pasta.

Stir Fry

Serves 4

This is great to make at the end of the week to use up all of your vegetables. I listed ingredients below that I typically use, but I like to switch it up and use different vegetables and proteins. You can serve this over rice or pasta.

Ingredients

3 T sesame oil
2-3 cloves of garlic
Head of broccoli
Few leaves of bok choy chopped
1 carrot, sliced
½ purple onion, sliced
1 red pepper, sliced
2 T Braggs organic coconut liquid aminos
A small piece of ginger, peeled and sliced
1 lb. chicken cooked, or other protein
A pinch of Vitamin L ❤

Directions

1. Heat sesame seed oil, add chopped garlic, then cook until light brown.
2. Add veggies, ginger and chicken toss.
3. Add Braggs organic coconut liquid aminos.

Serve over pasta or rice

Veggie Fried Rice

Serves 4

This is another good recipe for the end of the week to use up your vegetables. You can add protein to this recipe.

Ingredients

2 cups brown rice
1 cups broccoli, small pieces
½ cup carrot, chopped
1 cup baby spinach
½ cup onion
2 T garlic, chopped
2 T sesame oil
2 eggs, beaten
Braggs organic coconut liquid aminos
½ cup cashews
2-3 scallions, sliced
A spoonful of Vitamin L ❤

Directions

1. Heat oil in large pan and add garlic.
2. Add vegetables.
3. Add rice and mix.
4. Make a hole in center of pan by pushing vegetables to the side.
5. Add a touch of oil.
6. Add eggs and scramble.
7. Mix all together.
8. Sprinkle with Braggs organic coconut liquid aminos.

* Garnish with cashews and scallions (optional)

Sushi

Serves 3

I enjoy making sushi at home and coming up with new ideas to put in the seaweed wraps. An added bonus is you don't have to worry about all the added sugar that is in the sauces and rice when you go out.

Ingredients

6 sheets nori seaweed
1 cucumber, cut into thin slices
2 avocados, sliced into thin pieces
Salmon (or other protein)
Braggs organic coconut liquid aminos for dipping
Garnish with Vitamin L ❤

Optional Ingredients

Brown rice made with rice vinegar
Quinoa
Sesame seeds
Carrots
Herbs
Wasabi

Directions

1. Place nori seaweed sheet shiny side down on a clean and dry cutting board.

2. Layer the ingredients you are using and leave an inch open at the top.

3. Grab the corner that is open, lift up and roll.

4. When you get to the final inch of the seaweed, wet fingertips and apply to the nori sheet to seal roll closed.

5. Cut into equal parts using a sharp knife.

Pesto Sauce

This is a great recipe to prep ahead of time and either refrigerate or freeze. Pesto sauce is great on pasta but you can also use it on a variety of other things such as served on top of rice, scrambled eggs or toast.

Ingredients

2-3 cups fresh basil
½ cup olive oil
1/3 cup roasted nuts - pine, almonds, walnuts or cashews
3 cloves of garlic
Juice of ½ lemon
1 T nutritional yeast
Salt and pepper to taste
Pasta of choice
Lots of Vitamin L ❤

Directions

1. Add nuts and pulse.

2. Add the rest of the ingredients and pulse until well blended.

3. Serve over pasta or another grain.

Honey Lime Chicken

Ingredients

1 lb. chicken
¼ cup organic chicken broth
3 T olive oil
Juice of 2 limes
2 t organic raw honey
3 cloves garlic, minced
1 t cumin
2 T Braggs organic coconut liquid aminos
Garnish with Vitamin L ❤

Directions

1. Whisk together the chicken broth, olive oil, juice from limes, honey, garlic and cumin to make marinade.

2. Place marinade and chicken in a bowl or zip-lock bag and put in the refrigerator for at least an hour.

3. Pour into pan and broil under medium heat for 8-10 minutes.

Spicy Sweet Potato Fries

Serves 4-6

These are such a treat! You can use a variety of different seasonings on these, for example old bay, garlic or you can put cinnamon on them and dip them in maple syrup.

Ingredients

4 sweet potatoes, peeled and cut into ¼ inch pieces
2 T organic corn starch
1 T avocado oil
1 T coconut oil
½ t cayenne pepper
½ t thyme
Salt, pepper and Vitamin L to taste ❤

Directions

1. Preheat oven to 450.
2. Line baking sheet with parchment paper.
3. Place cut sweet potatoes in a zip-lock bag or bowl add corn starch and shake.
4. Pour into a strainer to remove excess cornstarch.
5. Place potatoes back in the bag or bowl and add oils and seasonings.
6. Shake and then place on the sheet.
7. Line the potatoes on the sheet and bake for 15 minutes then rotate and back for 10 more minutes.

Soups for the Creative Soul

Soups are so great to have in for a quick meal for either lunch or dinner. Below are a few of my favorite recipes but I also get creative with them. Sometimes I like to make my soups later in the week and use up any of my vegetables so they don't get wasted. For example, spinach is always a great one to add to any of the soups.

Carrot Ginger Cashew Soup with a Twist

Serves 3

Summer or winter it doesn't matter. I love eating soup. One time I was all set to make this soup and realized I only had vanilla-flavored coconut milk in the house, so I used it and loved the twist the vanilla flavor added to the soup. Now I always use vanilla coconut milk or add a splash of vanilla to the recipe.

Ingredients

1 lb. carrots
1 cup raw or unsalted cashews
32 oz. chicken or vegetable stock
½ cup vanilla flavored coconut milk (or regular coconut milk with splash of vanilla)
2 T fresh ginger, peeled and chopped
1 t onion powder
1/8 t garlic powder
Pinch of salt
Watercress and scallions for garnish
A spoonful of Vitamin L ❤

Directions

1. Pour stock in large pot, add carrots, cashews, chopped ginger, garlic and onion powder.

2. Bring to a boil.

3. Lower heat and let simmer for 20 minutes — test carrots for tenderness.

4. Add to blender or vita mixer.

5. Then add coconut milk and a pinch of salt.

6. Blend the ingredients.

7. Garnish with watercress and scallions.

Chicken, Beans and Greens Soup

Serves 6

This so good for you and delicious too. My kids like to add brown rice or quinoa (that I prepared ahead of time) to their soup when they are reheating.

Ingredients

2 T olive oil
½ t poultry seasoning
1 bunch kale, washed and chopped
4 stalks celery, washed and chopped
1 large onion, chopped
1 lb. carrots, washed and chopped
1 small clamshell container of organic spinach
1 lb. organic chicken breast cooked
2 cans cannellini beans
48 oz. chicken broth
Salt and pepper to taste
A dose of Vitamin L ❤

Directions

1. Heat the oil in a large pot on medium heat.

2. Add the chopped onion, celery, carrots and cook until tender

3. Add chicken broth and poultry seasoning, put heat on high and bring to a boil.

4. Reduce heat and add chicken, spinach, kale and beans.

5. Simmer for 20 minutes.

6. Add salt and pepper to taste.

Salad Dressings

I have been making homemade dressing for years, and I can't go back to the fake-tasting dressings. The store-bought salad dressings have so much added sugar and other nasty things. I even bring my dressings out to restaurants. If I am in a rush and don't have time to make the dressing I simply drizzle a little vinegar, oil and salt, and pepper on my salad. If I am out and get a salad and don't have my dressing, I ask for vinegar and oil. Or recently, I have found that more and more restaurants make their own dressings. If this is the case you can ask them for the ingredients.

Honey Lime Avocado Dressing/Dip

This is a nice creamy dressing that I sometimes use as a dip too. It is thick enough to dip fruits and veggies into.

Ingredients

1 ripe avocado
Juice of 1 lime
¼ cup olive oil
1 t apple cider vinegar
1 t honey
Dash of salt
A few drops of water and a few drops of Vitamin L ❤

Directions

1. Peel avocado and deseed.

2. Juice lime.

3. Place all ingredients in blender and blend until creamy.

Apple Maple Vinaigrette Dressing

This dressing goes well with a spinach salad with goat cheese and I also like to use it on the colorful salad.

Ingredients

2/3 cup olive oil
1/3 cup apple cider vinegar
2 T maple syrup
1 t Dijon mustard
Salt and pepper to taste
Add Vitamin L as needed ❤

Directions

1.   Place all the ingredients in the blender and blend until smooth.

Snacks

Snacking can often get a bad rap but I believe snacks are an important part of our day. We all know things can fall apart quickly when we get hungry and have nothing healthy around to eat. That is why being prepared ahead of time with healthy snacks is important. Prepare fruits, veggies and smoothies ahead of time or have some trail mix or nuts in your bag or car in case you get hungry. A snack in the afternoon can give you energy and also prevent you from over-eating at dinner time. Below are a few of my favorite snack recipes.

Lemon Garlic Hummus

Serves 4

This is a basic hummus recipe but you can get fancy and experiment with creating different flavors such as cilantro lime, roasted red pepper, Kalamata olive, horseradish.

Ingredients

1 15 oz. can chick peas, drained
¼ cup olive oil
Juice of 1 lemon
3 cloves garlic
½ t cumin
Salt, pepper and Vitamin L to taste ❤

Directions

1. Place all ingredients into blender and blend until smooth.
2. Chill before serving.

Fresh Popped Popcorn

Serves 2

You can experiment with adding different flavors to the popcorn such as old bay, cinnamon, cacao and pumpkin pie spice.

Ingredients

½ cup organic popcorn kernels
3 T olive oil or coconut oil
Sea salt to taste
A sprinkle of Vitamin L ❤

Directions

1. Place all ingredients in a brown paper lunch bag.
2. Fold over twice.
3. Microwave on high at least for a minute and half depending on microwave.

Chili Lime Cashews

Serves 6

This recipe is great with cashews; however you can also substitute other nuts or seeds.

Ingredients

4 cups unsalted cashews (or other nuts)
Juice of 3 limes
1 T lime zest, grated
1 T olive oil or coconut oil
2 t raw organic honey
2 T chili powder
1 t sea salt
A dose of Vitamin L ❤

Directions

1. Preheat oven to 250.
2. Line baking sheet with parchment paper.
3. In a large bowl whisk together lime juice, lime zest, oil, honey, chili powder and salt.
4. Add cashews and mix.
5. Place on baking sheet and bake for 20-25 minutes.
6. Store nuts in an airtight container.

Trail Mix

Serves 6

Trail mix is so quick and easy to make and also easy to get creative with and experiment. You can add different nuts, seeds or dried fruits. I love cherries and also love that I can find unsweetened dried cherries at Trader Joe's.

Ingredients

1 ½ cups raw cashews or mix of other nuts
1 cup pumpkin or sunflower seeds
½ cup cocoa nibs or vegan chocolate chips
½ cup unsweetened dried cherries 1 cup fresh popped popcorn
½ t cinnamon
Sea salt optional
Vitamin L not optional ❤

Directions

1. Combine all ingredients in a large bowl and mix.
2. Store in an airtight container.

Sweet Treats

Below are some of my favorite sweet treat recipes to make for special occasions or to have in if you need a little sweet treat. I already mentioned I like to follow the 80/20 rule, so a weekly sweet treat always makes me happy and keeps me from feeling deprived. They are free of refined sugar but still taste delicious. I have brought some of these treats to parties and gatherings and have received so many compliments. You can't even taste the difference. Eat your sweet treats slowly and enjoy every morsel.

Cashew Butter Balls

Makes about 2 dozen

I love these! One of my favorite things as a kid was tasting the cookie dough batter that my grandmom made. Well, these bring back that memory, and they taste like cookie dough!

In case you haven't noticed by now, I love cashews and for a good reason. Cashews have many health benefits. They are good for bone health, help with brain function and, my favorite benefit: they help boost your mood because they are high in tryptophan which helps increase levels of serotonin — the happy chemical.

You can also substitute other nut butters in this recipe such as almond or peanut butter.

Ingredients

1 ½ cups of gluten-free quick cooking oats
¼ cup flaxseed
¼ cup hemp seeds
Pinch of salt
½ cup creamy cashew butter
3 T honey
3 T maple syrup
½ cup vegan chocolate chips, cocoa nibs, raisins, nuts or unsweetened cherries (optional)
Pinch of Vitamin L ❤

Directions

1. Mix together all dry ingredients.

2. Then add wet ingredients and mix.

3. Form into 1-inch balls.

Raw Chocolate Mousse - Thrive Market

Serves 4

This mousse is decadent and always satisfies my chocolate craving.

Ingredients

2 cups pitted Medjool dates
2 cups almond or coconut milk
1 T chia seeds
8 T cacao powder
¼ cup cashew butter
½ t sea salt
1 ½ t vanilla extract
A spoonful of Vitamin L ❤

Directions

1. Soak the dates and almond milk together in a bowl for 3 hours.

2. Transfer to a high-speed blender and blend on high until creamy.

3. Add the chia seeds, cocoa powder, cashew butter, salt and vanilla and blend until well mixed.

4. Pour into ramekins and top with nuts and berries, or other fruit as desired.

Granola

Serves 6

Like the trail mix, granola is another recipe with which you can really let your creative spirit come out and play! You can enjoy this granola plain or serve it with berries, unsweetened coconut yogurt or almond or coconut milk.

Ingredients

2 cups raw cashews
2 cups raw walnuts
1 cup raw pumpkin seeds
1 cup unsweetened dried cherries
1 cup raw slivered almonds
¼ cup coconut oil, melted
1 ½ t ground cinnamon
1 T ground flaxseed
4 T water
¼ cup maple syrup or honey
1 t vanilla extract
Sea salt and Vitamin L to taste ❤

Directions

1. Preheat the oven to 300 degrees.

2. In a medium bowl mix the flaxseed and water. Let stand for 10 minutes.

3. In a large bowl mix together the first 5 ingredients.

4. In the medium bowl add the coconut oil, maple syrup, vanilla extract, ground cinnamon and salt then whisk together.

5. Pour over the combination in the large bowl and mix well.

6. Spread the granola on a large baking sheet for 20 minutes.

7. Stir mixture and bake for 5-10 more minutes.

8. Remove the granola from the oven and let sit for 10 minutes.

9. Break the pieces up using a spatula.

10. Store in an airtight container.

Oatmeal Cookies

Makes 12-18 cookies

When I make these I usually double the batter and freeze some of the cookies; my daughter loves to heat them in the microwave for breakfast.

Ingredients

½ cup cassava flour
½ cup brown rice flour
1/3 cup oat flour (or you can experiment with any mix of gluten-free flours)
2 T flaxseed
1 t baking soda
1 t baking powder
1 t cinnamon
Dash of sea salt
½ cup coconut sugar
1/3 cup maple syrup
2 eggs
½ cup coconut oil
¼ cup avocado oil
2 t vanilla
2 ½ cups gluten-free oats
3/4 cup of raisins, vegan chocolate chips or dried cherries
Add Vitamin L as needed ❤

Directions

1. Preheat oven to 375.

2. Mix all dry ingredients in a bowl.

3. Mix together all dry ingredients.

4. In another bowl, mix together the oils, sugar, maple syrup, egg and vanilla.

5. Add the dry ingredients to the wet mix.

6. Mix in the dry oats and raisins, chip, cherries, etc.

7. Refrigerate batter for at least an hour.

8. Line cookie sheet with parchment paper and drop dough on cookie sheet.

9. Bake for about 8 minutes - ovens may vary so could be longer.

Dark Chocolate Almond Bark

This makes a big batch of chocolate. I store it in the refrigerator or freezer and grab a piece or two for my chocolate fix. You can also make it with cashews or other nuts.

Ingredients

1 cup coconut oil
6 T maple syrup
1 cup cacao powder
1 cup almond slivers or crushed almonds
Sea salt and Vitamin L to taste ❤

Directions

1. Melt coconut oil in saucepan on medium.

2. Add cocoa and maple syrup.

3. Stir until all ingredients are blended.

4. Add ¾ cup of the almonds and a touch of sea salt to taste.

5. Pour into a 13x9 sheet pan.

6. Top with the rest of the almonds and sea salt.

7. You can also add other toppings such as shredded coconut raisins, etc.

8. Place in the freezer for at least 30 minutes.

9. Then break into pieces and enjoy!

10. Store extra in an airtight refrigerator.

11. You can also use this recipe to make candy molds instead of using a sheet pan.

Iced Cashew Coffee

Serves 1

Sipping this drink makes me feel like I am at a quaint coffee place and it is a great dose of self-care for me. I love making it for my friends when they stop by for a cup of coffee.

Ingredients

½ cup boiling water
½ cup raw or unsalted cashews
½ cup coconut milk
½ cup coffee at room temperature (I usually put an extra coffee I have left over in the pot in the refrigerator so I have it in for this drink)
1 t coconut sugar (or other sweetener of choice)
½ t pure vanilla extract
Ice and Vitamin L ❤

Directions

1. Boil water and pour on top of the cashews.

2. Let soak for 20 minutes to soften the cashews.

3. Then place all the ingredients in the blender and blend.

Hot Chocolate with Coconut Whipped Cream

Serves 2

This hot chocolate is tasty on a cold winter day. There will be leftover whipped cream. You can save this and eat it with berries for another delicious treat.

Ingredients

2 cups coconut milk
2 T cacao powder
2 T coconut sugar
A splash pure vanilla extract and Vitamin L ❤

Directions

1. Heat the coconut milk in a large pot and bring to a boil.

2. Turn heat to low and add the rest of the ingredients and stir well.

Coconut Whipped Cream

Serves 6

This is so creamy and tastes delicious on top of your hot chocolate. You can also serve it with berries or granola.

Ingredients

1 15 oz can coconut cream (full fat)
1 T organic maple syrup or raw honey
1 t vanilla
Vitamin L to warm the soul ❤

Directions

1. Refrigerate the can of coconut cream overnight and place a stainless-steel bowl and the beaters in the freezer for an hour before making.

2. Open can and separate the thick consistency from and the water consistency. You will be using the thick consistency for the whipped cream.

You can save the watery part and use it in your morning smoothie or coffee.

3. Place the thick consistency in a stainless steel bowl and mix on high until it yields a light and fluffy consistency.

4. Add the maple syrup and vanilla and beat again

Creative Meal Planning

Week of _____

Add color to your plate - add color to your world!

Dinner for the Week:

Monday: _____

Tuesday: _____

Wednesday: _____

Thursday: _____

Friday: _____

Saturday: _____

Sunday: _____

Grocery List:

Breakfast Ideas: **Lunch Ideas:**   **Smoothie Ideas:**

Grains: **Proteins:**   **Snacks/Treats:**   **Salads:**   **Other:**

Creative Meal Planning

Week of _____

Add color to your plate - add color to your world!

Dinner for the Week:

Monday: *Pasta/Veggies Cream Sauce Chick Pea Salad*

Tuesday: *Cashew Ginger Soup with watercress and scallions and side salad*

Wednesday: *Pesto Sauce over Pasta or other grain Grilled Chicken*

Thursday: *Stir Fry with Protein*

Friday: *Tacos and Guacamole*

Saturday: *Go out*

Sunday: *Salmon and Veggies*

Grocery List:

Basil
Cucumbers
Avocado
Scallions
Watercress
Grape Tomatoes
Veggies for Stir Fry
Chicken
Grass Fed Meat
Ingredients for Tacos

Breakfast Ideas:
Hardboiled Eggs
Smoothie
Flaxseed muffin
Chia Jar – choc banana

Lunch Ideas:
Chick Pea Salad
Leftovers on top of salad

Smoothie Ideas:
Basil Detox
Salted Choc Cashew

Grains:	Proteins:	Snacks/Treats:	Salads:	Other:
Quinoa Pasta	*Hardboiled Eggs*	*Oatmeal Cookies*	*Chick Pea Salad*	*Pesto Sauce*
	Grilled Chicken	*Honey Lime Dip*		
	Raw Veggies			

*Please note – the grocery list is only a sampling of items you will need for the week.

Creative Meal Planning

Week of _____

Add color to your plate - add color to your world!

Dinner for the Week:

Monday: Rotisserie Chicken Roasted Veggies

Tuesday: Chicken, Beans and Greens Soup (use leftover chicken from Monday)

Wednesday: Salmon Cakes and Veggies

Thursday: Sushi with Salmon Sautéed Spinach

Friday: Go out

Saturday: Veggie Fried Rice

Sunday: Honey Lime Chicken, Sweet Potato Fries and Colorful Salad

Grocery List:

Kale

Spinach

Cilantro

Cucumbers

Avocado

Brown Rice

Pinto Beans

Cannellini Beans

Chicken

Salmon

Seaweed

Breakfast Ideas:
Egg Muffins
Chia Jar - Pumpkin Spice
Oatmeal

Lunch Ideas:
Brown Rice Salad
Salmon cake over salad

Smoothie Ideas:
Tropical Summer
Green Love

Grains:
Brown Rice

Proteins:
Nuts/Trail Mix
Chicken

Snacks/Treats:
Choc Mousse
Hummus

Salads:
Brown Rice Salad

Other:

*Please note – the grocery list is only a sampling of items you will need for the week.

170

Give meal planning a try. I think you will be very happy with the results. You can create four weekly meal plans and rotate them. This time spent ahead of time will create openings in your life.

However, living in the flow of life is key here. There will be days or weeks when the detours of life happen and we don't always get to the things we plan on doing like meal planning. But remember that detours are different than distracting yourself.

Always try to take that action towards your next goal, but also remember that you are human.

"A goal without a plan is just a wish."

- Antoine de Saint-Exupery

#7

BE BOLD-BE BRAVE-BE YOU!

Go with the Flow

"Be brave enough to live your life creatively."

- Alan Alda

On a whim, I signed up for a paint night my business networking group was hosting. As I clicked the button to pay, I was a little hesitant and unsure. I had never painted on canvas before.

I showed up and my spot was all set up for me — a canvas on an easel, a palette of paint, water and brushes.

"I can't do this," I said to myself.

But next thing you know I was creating on canvas.

We were painting a tree with swirly branches and a gold background. On the branches of the tree, we could paint symbols of things that we wanted to bring into our lives.

The instructor gave us guidelines yet told us to use our intuition to guide us while we were painting.

I followed her advice and did things a little differently than the directions. I glanced around at the other paintings. They were so different from mine but I felt that my painting was a reflection of me and I didn't need to compare myself. I stepped out of my comfort zone a little more and kept painting.

This painting is now displayed in a place in my house where I can view it every day. It reminds me to step out of my comfort zone on a daily basis. I am grateful that I signed up for this art class. This activity helped me break down some barriers inside. I never knew I had the ability to paint inside of me.

This story is from a male friend who attended one of my workshops. Most of my workshops are filled with women, but I have also had a handful of men. I have observed that the men usually seem to come into the paint workshops with more confidence than the woman participants. They don't come in and say that they can't do it; they take action immediately. I love this story and am glad that my friend shared with me how much he learned about himself during a two and half-hour workshop. Over the years I have compiled so many lessons I learned from painting. I also continue to learn from others when I teach them how to paint.

Lessons 1 Learned from Painting

The males in my workshop remind me to be bold. I remember back to one of my first lessons with Karl Kuerner. There were several other people in the class, and we were all creating our own paintings. I had a picture of my daughter in her Easter dress that I wanted to paint.I had this idea to paint her standing in a field of flowers in front of a picket fence. My imagination could picture it perfectly but I sat there paralyzed with fear. My shadow voice was so loud and it was convincing me that I couldn't begin my painting until I was given instructions. Karl came over and said, "Just be bold and aggressive, get some paint on the canvas."

"Painting isn't rocket science," he would say over and over to his students, "Pick up the brush and start."

All of a sudden something shifted in me and I was able to begin this painting of my daughter. I still heard my shadow voice, but it became fainter as I picked up the brush and added paint to the canvas. "You can't mess up," I heard my intuitive voice say.

Just take action, be bold — this is a lesson I can take with me in my life. Don't be paralyzed and overthink things. Our shadow voice will always be there, as will our intuitive voice.

As I start a new painting, I always say to myself, "Just get that first layer down." The fear I once had of starting a painting is easier now because I remember those words from that lesson with Karl. Sure, I still hear my shadow voice saying I can't do this each time, but each time I make a bold move to add a layer on the canvas, it seems like I unravel a layer of myself. This unraveling takes me deeper into my inner world where I can become my own authority and can create my world.

As I continued to work on this painting of my daughter in class I learned more lessons. I poured some green paint and started the grass in the field. Karl encouraged me to use other colors in the grass, like black, shades of yellow and some orange. He said, "Look at nature, you don't see straight green." I learned to look at nature differently, and I saw all the colors nature had to offer. I found beauty everywhere, and painting helped me appreciate the world more fully.

"You can't mess up!" Karl would repeat over and over in class. I use acrylic paint as my medium and it is so forgiving. You can go back and paint over any so-called "mistakes." I applied this lesson to my life and saw that I could go back in my life and reframe things that happened, not deny them but accept the things that happened and forgive my so-called "mistakes" and the past.

Making Room for the Dark

Karl wasn't one to teach a lot of technique; his style of teaching was geared towards guiding us to listen to our intuitive voice while painting and then he would point out certain techniques. However, he wanted us to understand the concept of lights and darks. If there is one technique you should understand before you start a painting, this would be it. He would always say, "Get your dark in first and then you can get to the light. The dark defines the light." In this painting I was doing of my daughter, Karl encouraged me to get the dark grass in first. So I used dark green and black to do the first layer of grass. Then Karl said, "Add the light of the grass and the flowers. The dark makes everything else pop," he stated.

Over the years I learned that a painting couldn't exist without darks. At first, I felt so uncomfortable putting all that dark paint on the canvas; it didn't seem right. Karl would always say, "Trust me." I realized this was symbolic of life. Nothing exists without its opposite here on earth, so how could I exist without darkness? It can feel very uncomfortable facing the darkness. However, I learned to embrace the darkness – which includes our shadow voice, our weaknesses, our buried stories, and all the things we want to deny or defend. Accepting all the darkness helps us find the light and leads us to a life full of meaning and passion.

I learned more from this one painting of my daughter in her Easter dress that I created under the guidance of Karl than I would have ever learned in art school.

I encourage you to start creating not as a means to get a finished product but to get to know yourself better.

Angela in Flower Land

A Work in Progress

While studying with Karl, I attended critique sessions with the other students. Sometimes I felt very vulnerable bringing my unfinished paintings to these sessions. I remember one student critiquing my painting and saying, "You have branches on the trees that are on the right of the painting, but where are the branches of your trees to the left?"

I wanted to say to her, "Well no duh, I'm not finished yet." But I calmly said, "I didn't get to that part of the painting yet."

At first, I felt like I went to so many of these sessions trying to justify or defend that I wasn't done with my painting. A part of me was also thinking shouldn't we all realize this, we are all bringing works in progress to the critique session? But then as time went on, I realized that, like all of us, I was a work in progress and, like these unfinished paintings, I wasn't finished yet. I was still learning, always learning and I could share myself with the world even though I wasn't perfect or finished. This was such a freeing experience.

Create What You Want to Bring Into Your Life

I learned that I could bring things into my life by painting and sketching. Of course, the way I learned this was by sheer accident. Here's the story –

For as long as I can remember, my daughter relentlessly begged for a dog. I think "dog" was her first word. As she got older, she would look online, research types of dogs and ask us to take her to dog shelters to find a dog. She drew pictures of the dog she wanted and hung them all over the house.

Now, I have nothing against dogs. I had them growing up and loved them but wasn't sure if I wanted to take on the responsibility of owning one as an adult.

One day I said to her, "I know, how about I paint you a picture of a dog?" She laughed and said," Yes, but I still want a real one, too."

So, on a cold November night, I started a painting called Welcome Home. It was a nighttime snow scene, with a house and path to the house. My daughter and son were walking up the path, and a dog was running to greet them. My daughter loved it. In fact, I think this gave her more momentum. Her campaign for a dog became even stronger. She spent countless hours online, trying to figure out which type of dog would be best for us. She decided upon a Morkie (Maltese and Yorkie mix).

One weekend, the local pet shop had a Morkie up for adoption, so next thing you know we were there meeting this dog. They weren't sure of the dog's age; they thought he was six. All I know is he was crazy, chasing the other dogs, biting them and going to the bathroom everywhere in the store. There was no way; I was ready to bring this dog home. My daughter pouted as we left the pet store.

But this didn't stop her. We went home and she got back on the computer and announced that a pet store a few towns over just got some Morkies. "Can we look at them please?" she begged. I reluctantly agreed and said to her, "We will look, but we are NOT leaving with a dog!"

She jumped out of the car when we got there, ran right up to the salesperson, and asked him where the Morkies were. He walked us over to their cage, and I saw the look of disappointment on her face. These Morkies were black, and she wanted a lighter colored one. This girl sure had a clear picture in her mind of what she wanted. The salesperson said, "There are some light colored Morkies at the other location."

Next thing you know, we were in the car driving across town to the other location. We walked in, and she spotted two of them that she loved. One was mild, and one was wild. The sales person took us to the play area and let us spend time with each of them.

The wild one immediately took a liking to us; he licked my face and neck and snuggled into me like he had found his home. The salesman said they were running a special that day. I got my bearings together and said firmly, "We are only looking today; we are NOT leaving with a dog!"

Well to make a long story short, we did leave with a dog - the wild one.

For some reason this salesperson wanted us to have this dog. He kept cutting the price and even started throwing other items in on the deal. It was the eve of Valentine's Day, so he said, "I will give you a red coat for him."

Just like that, we had a new addition to our family. A few days later my daughter noticed the painting that I had created for her. 'Mom, look," she said, "The dog you painted looks just like Cody, and he even has a red coat." I also realized that I created this painting in November, right near the day our bundle of energy was born.

Hmm ... maybe I should start painting what I want in my life. I thought to myself as I stared at the painting.

Welcome Home

Wow ... Did my daughter's focused energy and drawings and my painting somehow bring this cute little furry friend into our lives or was it just by chance? There was something to this, I knew it, and so I started experimenting with it. I began painting, sketching and doodling what I wanted to bring into my life. I started using this technique with friends and clients. We didn't always paint; many times we drew little sketches. I found it particularly useful when it was done at night or early in the morning.

I called this technique Dream Doodles, and you can try it for yourself. It is explained in the activity section below.

Activities

1. Practice Dream Doodles

Step 1

Get a journal for your sketches and doodles .

Step 2

Get clear on something you want to bring into your life. Maybe you desire a new job, love, a dog, or money. Yes, it is okay to draw money or symbols for abundance. Drawing money symbols doesn't mean that a pound of sliced thin twenties will fall from the sky. Focusing your energy can shift things; for example, my one friend painted a money tree and shortly after someone came into her life to help her get her finances in order.

Step 3

First thing in the morning or at night take five minutes to sketch or doodle; you can draw symbols or pictures. I have found that this is a good activity to do when you are feeling happy. Who cares what they look like … just be free. You can also add in words. Remember when you were a kid, the good feeling you felt when you doodled in class.

It is that simple … now, this is not to say that things always work out how we want. However, it feels good to put your energy towards something you want; it seems to change your mindset.

Step 4

This is the important step: let go of the outcome. Let the universe work its magic.

2. Be Bold and Creative in all Areas of Your Life

Do things you usually wouldn't do, for example —

- Wear something you usually wouldn't wear
- Eat something you usually wouldn't eat
- Go somewhere you usually wouldn't go
- Listen to music you usually wouldn't listen to
- Create a new recipe

"When you want something you never had,

you have to do something you have never done."

- Paulo Coelho

#8

BREAK THE RIGHT RULES

Wild Child

"If a man [woman] does not keep pace with his companions,

perhaps it is because he hears a different drummer.

Let him step to the music which he hears,

however measured or far away."

\- Henry David Thoreau

I take a deep breath. No matter how organized I am, it always seems to get a little hectic as I am setting up for a paint party. I ground myself before I leave for my paint party with a walk in the grass and I always take time to meditate for the people who will be attending. I pray that they can be bold and let their creative spirit come out and be alive.

As I am pouring the rainbow of colors on the palette, people start strolling in. The same conversation always seems to replay.

"WHAT!! You expect me to paint that!" someone will shout as they spot the painting we will be creating. "You are crazy! I can't even draw a straight line!"

They say this as if they never saw the painting that was posted in the advertisement when they signed up for the paint party.

I answer them by saying, "Tonight you will paint your version of this painting. I will be your guide on the side, and I promise I will walk you step by step through the painting."

But they still fight it a little. "You never saw me draw; I am awful," they insist. "I can't even draw a stick figure."

They will repeat this over and over to the other people sitting at their table. Every time it seems that halfway through the night something shifts for them and they settle into a calm and meditative state while painting.

Interestingly enough, this person is always a woman. As I stated in the previous chapter the men come right in and take action, which reminds me to be bold in life. The women remind that it is okay to release an uncomfortable feeling — a perfect combination for creativity.

I started teaching these types of painting workshops over ten years ago, first with kids and then with adults. Now I teach all ages to pick up that brush and take that bold first stroke on the canvas.

"What is the worst that can happen?" I ask before we start painting. "You make a so-called 'mistake'?" I go on to explain, "It isn't a mistake, it is just experimenting, and it is a way of learning and moving forward."

184

People thought I was crazy when I first started teaching these workshops. Well-meaning friends said to me, "Not everyone can paint on canvas." As if painting on canvas is only for a select few.

By now we know that is not true.

I explained to my well-meaning friends that all you need to paint on canvas is a willingness or desire. Directions that are broken down into small steps for you and someone who believes in you.

At each paint party I tell the attendees that I will break down the process into small steps for them. I tell them that I taught kindergarten, so I am good at this. Someone always laughs and says, "Good, because my art is like a kindergartner."

I respond, "Great, that is what I want to see. Kindergarten kids have freedom when it comes to painting."

I also tell them another important factor is having someone believe in them as they paint. I assure all the attendees that I will believe in all of them tonight as they create their masterpieces. I trust that there is an "Art Spirit" in each of us; sometimes it is buried under a lot of stories and disbelief, but it is there.

Then I proceed to read the following quote by Howard Ikemoto I have posted in front of the room:

"When my daughter was about seven years old, she asked me one day what I did at work. I told her I worked at the college – that my job was to teach people how to draw. She stared back at me, incredulously, and said, 'You mean they forget?'"

Sharing this quote always elicits a laugh or two, and it appears as if people begin to breathe deeper and feel a sense of freedom. A little shift in energy has occurred.

Then they pick up their brushes, dip them in the colorful palette and the journey to their inner art spirit begins. I guide them and tell them to let their intuition also be the guide. "As you are painting, allow ideas to come to you for ways you can add to or change the painting. Make it your own." I tell them.

I emphasize that creativity is a place where you can break some rules; be defiant when you are painting.

By the end of the paint night, people leave with a finished masterpiece that was a blank canvas only a few hours before. Many of them have added their own touches to their paintings; each canvas holds a unique story.

Speaking of unique stories — before one paint party, I received a text from one of the attendees who had been to prior paint nights. It was a Halloween-themed paint night and we were painting a pumpkin patch. She asked in her text if she could paint a psychedelic kitty instead of a pumpkin patch. Requests like this make me smile; I love when people march to beat of their own drum. She proudly displayed her painting as we took a picture of everyone at the end of the paint party. Everyone holding their pumpkin patch paintings (which were unique in their own right) and there she was proudly holding her psychedelic kitty.

Ironically, that same person who expresses at the beginning of the paint party that they have no creativity is always the last one still painting. They don't seem to want the experience to end. They are content and calm. I tell them they don't have to rush and that they can keep painting as I am cleaning up. Finally though, I share with them a quote that Karl learned from Andrew Wyeth, a quote he always shared with his students at the end of a painting. "It takes two people to do a painting, one to paint it and the other to hit you over the head to tell you that you are done." Our perfectionist can come into play, and we want to keep going, but at one point we have to finish the painting so we can move on.

Breaking the right rules is another lesson I learned from painting. Too many rules stifle creativity. I remember on one particular occasion, Karl looked at one of my paintings and said that my painting didn't follow any of the rules or techniques that the masters would say to do. But then he quickly replied, "You seem to have a way of breaking the rules when painting and you somehow get away with it."

I think it is because I have been questioning and breaking the right rules since I was a kid. Not the rules that are meant to help us or keep us safe, like stopping at a red light or not texting while you're driving. I like to question the kind of rules that keep us from living or keep us from being who we came here to be. For example, you can't wear white until after Memorial Day, or never eat after 8:00 pm or you should wait six months to date after you get divorced, or if your child isn't talking by a year and a half you need to start worrying.

As a child and as a teacher, I questioned the rules in school. I questioned them because they didn't feel right to me. I recall one particular incident in my freshman year in high school.

> *Dressed in a dark blue jumper, light blue blouse, knee socks and saddle shoes, I crossed my arms in defiance.*
>
> *"No, I am not going today," I said to my teacher, a nun.*
>
> *"It is mandatory confession; you have to go," she replied.*
>
> *"I am not going," I repeated.*
>
> *"Why not?" she asked.*
>
> *"I don't need to tell someone else my sins when I can talk God and tell him myself," I replied to her. I know Him, I thought to myself and I can talk to Him anytime I want.*
>
> *My mind flashed back to that night in the hospital, when I stayed up praying all night. I thought about how my mom taught me to pray. I spoke and prayed to God all the time, especially at night when I was safe in my bed. I told him my fears and worries. When I prayed I felt God's presence, I heard his whispers. His love surrounded me. I also felt His presence when I drew all the characters from books. I did know Him.*
>
> *"If you don't go to confession, I will have to give you demerits."*
>
> *The sound of the nun's voice jolted me back into the present.*

You think a few demerits will hurt me? I wanted to scream at her. Instead, with my arms still crossed I replied, "I will take the demerits; I am not going to confession."

This was the first of many demerits I received in high school, most of them for speaking up, for speaking a truth that was inside me. This nun seemed to get frustrated with me on many occasions, and she would often say to me, "You should take a page out of your sister's book!" My sister was in the grade above. Although this made everyone laugh, including myself, this often left me feeling so inferior and wondering what was wrong with my book, my stories and my pages.

My arms remained crossed through high school; they protected me. Art and the inner world I created through my drawings helped me survive.

For years, I carried shame inside around these stories of speaking up and going against the norm. I realize now it wasn't about being right or wrong. I see how I questioned rules when they didn't feel right to me. It was my intuitive voice guiding me.

From my experiences, I didn't feel safe with the priests, and I protected myself by not going to confession. On the other hand, my friend from childhood, the one who created Inspired Action Meditation with me, loved going to confession. She felt better after she shared with the priest. It is great to have discussions with her, without having to defend my choices and she doesn't feel the need to convince me that her way was right either. It helps clarify that there is no one-size-fits-all answer.

You can use the concept that there is no one-size-fits-all answer and apply it to all areas of your life - your relationships, how you raise your children, your religious and spiritual practices, marriages and partnerships, and your work. This simple practice can change your life.

Activities

"If you hear a voice inside you say that you cannot paint, then by all means paint, and that voice will be silenced."

- Vincent Van Gogh

1. Create a Bonfire Painting

Here is your chance to practice and to be bold and break some rules. At the end of this chapter you will find directions for a painting lesson that you can try at home. If you are a visual person like myself, you can find access to slide show directions with pictures here –

http://www.liveyourcreativity.com/book-landing-page/

Remember that the directions are only a set of guidelines, so listen to your intuition and be guided by your intuitive voice. Take this skill of listening to your intuitive voice into every area of your life.

Bonfire

Paint a painting that only you can create and live a life that only you can live. The paintbrush is in your hand, and your blank canvas is waiting. So be bold, be brave, be you!

2. Have a Real Bonfire and Burn all the Stories and Beliefs that No Longer Serve You

Take your creativity thieve stories and place them in the fire. Take the stories around your body image and burn those too. Replace these old stories with new ones and ignite the creative spark inside of you.

Sacred Ceremony

3. Experiment with Breaking the Right Rules in Your Life

In so many areas of our life, we have been programmed with these beliefs that someone just told us we should do. Make it a practice to question some of these beliefs when it comes to your relationships, how you raise your children and your religious and spiritual practices. So much of life is about conforming. Do something to break one of these programmed rules. For example, don't sign your child up for a million different activities just because everyone else is doing it. Listen to your intuition to see what works best for you, your child and your family. Try out a different church in your neighborhood if it feels right for you. Get creative when it comes to breaking the right rules.

"Live your life as an exclamation, not an explanation!"

- Isaac Newton

Directions for Creating Your Bonfire Painting

Created by Christine Burke

10 Steps to Create Your Own Masterpiece

Tools
11x14 canvas
Small round brush
Big round brush
Fan brush
2 paper plates
Cup of water
Baby wipe/paper towel
Small easel

Acrylic Paint Colors
White
Ultramarine blue
Viridian green
Yellow
Black
Red
Orange
Burnt sienna

Step 1 - Create your Painting Space

Set up all your materials and pour the paint colors on a paper plate. Pour a cup of water. I always love to light a candle, get a drink and put some things that I like in my creative space for example, a plant or some crystals, and some background music. Feel free to create your space however you would like. Take a deep breath before you begin and invite your "Art Spirit" in.

Step 2 - Horizontal Canvas

Place your canvas on the easel in a horizontal position. If you don't have an easel place it on a flat surface.

Step 3 - Grass line

Take your big round brush and dip it into the water and tap it on side of the cup to get excess water off (do this each time you dip your brush in water). Dip the tip of the brush into the edge of the green paint and drag a bit until you get a little bit of paint on your brush. Draw a straight green line across the canvas about a ¼ of the way up from the bottom.

Step 4 - The Night Sky

Take your fan brush and dip it into water. Then dip half of the tip of the brush in black and the other half of the tip of the brush in blue paint. Hold the brush at the end and cross hatch the white area above the green line to create the night sky.

Cross hatching is to shade or hatch with two or more sets of parallel lines that cross one another. It is like making a lot of X's with the paintbrush. Paint all the way down to the green line.

Note: After step 5, you can go back to the sky and do a second layer.

Step 5 - The Grass

Now you will paint the grass. Take your fan brush, dip it into the water. Then dip it in green, yellow and a little bit of black paints and paint in upward motions in the white area below the sky. Now add the second layer of the sky.

Step 6 - The Fire Pit

Now you are ready to paint the rocks. Find the middle of the canvas and go about two inches down from the grass line. Here we will begin painting the beginning of the first rock. The rocks are flat on the bottom and rounded on the top. Use the big round brush; for the rocks you will be using black paint, with touches of white to give them a gray look.

Next, do the outlines of the rocks in an oval shape. I have ten rocks but depending on how big you do your rocks and oval shape, you may have more or less.

Then fill in the rocks with black and a little bit of white paint. So that you can tell the difference of when one rock ends and another begins, you will use the technique of darks and lights, for example, make the end of one rock dark with all black and the rock next to it use a little white, so it looks gray.

Continue this pattern.

Then fill in the middle of the fire pit in all black.

Step 7 - The Fire

The fire is next. Dip your big round brush in yellow and orange and draw what looks like a sideways crescent moon at the bottom of the fire pit. Then rotate the following colors: red, white, yellow and orange and make squiggly lines coming up into the sky with the big round brush.

Hold the brush at the end and freely paint these squiggly lines. Do two layers. Try and keep the red and white away from each other or you will make pink.

Then rotate the following colors: red, white, yellow and orange and make squiggly lines coming up into the sky with the big round brush.

Hold the brush at the end and freely paint these squiggly lines. Do two layers. Try and keep the red and white away from each other or you will make pink.

Step 8 - The Sticks and Marshmallows

The sticks and marshmallows are next. Use your big round brush and dip it into the light brown and black. On the left side of the canvas start the stick about an inch above the grass line. Draw it on a diagonal and stop right before the fire. Do the same thing on the right side of the canvas.

Now you are ready for the marshmallows. Use the small round brush and white paint. Paint an oval near the end of the stick on the left. Paint two small straight lines coming up from the oval and then paint a curved line on top. Next, fill in the marshmallows with white and a little yellow paint. Shade the marshmallows on one side with gray paint, to make gray paint use white with a little bit of black. My marshmallows are a little different in size and shape. Feel free to do yours any way you choose.

Step 9 - Blades of Grass

Now you will add the extra blades of grass coming over the bottom of the rocks and into the sky area. Take your large round brush and dip it into the water. Then dip it into just a little bit of yellow and green and make quick upward sweeping motions.

Step 10 - Stars

The final step - the stars. For the stars, we will use the other end of the small round brush (the opposite of the brush) Dip the tip of in white and make stars on the canvas. Don't make them too big or don't do too many stars. Otherwise, it will wind up looking like snow.

FINAL THOUGHTS

Round and Round We Go

"Goodbye …??

Oh no, please can't we go back to page one

and do it all over again?"

- Winnie the Pooh

This isn't the end; it is just the beginning. The beginning of your journey of creating a rich inner life where you embrace your individual journey (the dark and the light) and realize that you don't have to starve yourself anymore. A life where you invite your "Art Spirit" to be with you at all times.

Thanks for sharing this journey with me; it has been an honor.

Back in November of 2017, once again I found myself on a whim signing up for another Institute for Integrative Nutrition® Class, this time it was the Launch Your Dream Book Program. What seemed like a whim was serendipity and my intuition guiding me to listen to my desires. Pay attention to the signs because they are everywhere!

I enjoyed writing this book so much; I didn't want it to end. But there were of course triumphs and tribulations along the way. It was so joyful at times to write, and other times I wanted to scream because I did things like typed for an hour and forgot to save my work.

My shadow voice yelled, "You are so disorganized," but my intuitive voice gently cheered me on and said you can do this, just keep going." I surrendered and was always guided to my next action. My shadow voice would get worried about the next twenty steps of writing a book. My intuitive voice thought of only the next step and enjoyed that step. This is how a book is written. This is how a meaningful life is lived — in the moment focusing on the present step.

As I wrote this book, I realized again that my book, my stories and my pages were perfect just the way they were and that I no longer needed to take a page out of my sister's book or anyone else's for that matter. I hope that from reading this book, you accept your stories and see that they were perfect in creating who you are and what you have to offer in life. Go and share your stories, paint your stories, create from your stories, love your stories and rewrite them where you feel it is necessary.

Just like a painting, I needed to be hit over the head to finish this book. I wanted it to be perfect but realized that expecting things to be perfect can hold us back at times. Then I remembered that the opposite of perfection is imperfect and flawed and I embraced them both. I have learned to accept the dark and the light, thus allowing me to be brave and bold in all areas of my life. So, go forth and be bold; life was meant to be lived to the fullest.

Where Do You Go from Here?

As Robert Henri states, "Don't close the book. Keep opening it ... there are still more pages."

Go back to page one and take the parts of the book that work for you. I have offered lots of activities for you to do. You don't have to do them all: remember bio-individuality.

Create your own individual program from these suggestions and seek out fellow travelers and collect allies along the way to share this journey with, someone you feel safe sharing all of your emotions with. Connect with your Guides on the other side and your loved ones who have gone before you. Feed your art spirit on a daily basis. Live a rich and creative life and don't starve yourself from all that life has to offer. Don't be a starving artist ... choose to be a well-nourished artist.

If you are looking for like-minded friends to hang out with, you can connect with me on FB at https://www.facebook.com/ChristinesArtWorldUS/ or join my FB group The Well-Nourished Artist. You can follow me on Instagram at https://www.instagram.com/christinesartworld/

I put together a list of reminders for you to take with you.

- Say no when you mean no.
- Don't be afraid to fire someone from your life.
- Remember to practice Gratitude with a Twist.
- Use Inspired Action Meditation to help you listen to your next inspired action.
- Do something every day for the inner artist no matter how small. Even if you just remember him/her while you are cooking. This inspires all of us and keeps the creative spirit alive.
- Remember don't put your creative being in a separate compartment and have him/her only show up when you are painting or writing. Invite this creative spirit everywhere you go. If we didn't have human experiences, we would have nothing to create.
- Next time you are feeling a human emotion that might feel uncomfort-

able, do something creative instead of reaching for food or alcohol; it gives you a high that will last.

- Eat whole foods.
- Be bold.
- Be Brave.
- Try something new.
- Do your morning pages.
- Create your own rituals.
- Practice pampering self-care intertwined with grown-up self-care.
- Share your emotions - all of them.
- Get angry but do it in a safe and healthy way for all.
- Have a good cry when you need one.
- Live, love and be like only you can
- Don't starve your body or your creative soul – nourish them both
- Don't fall prey to the external world - create a rich inner world.

I guess it is goodbye, for now. I would like to end this part of the journey with a poem.

This poem poured out of me many years ago, immediately after I fired the instructor that was draining my energy. It is amazing what happens in our lives when we are bold and do things that might seem so hard for us to do. We feel the fear and do it anyway.

I used canvas as my medium in the poem, but you can replace it with whatever you would like, such as a blank piece paper to write a song, story or recipe, a plate to create a meal … the options are endless.

Your canvas is waiting. Now go and create!

Creation by Christine Burke

My studio waits patiently
for a creative soul to come and play.
Slowly I enter and sit and stare
at the blank vastness of white that lies before me.

Overwhelmed I want to run,
but I somehow convince myself to stay.
Art spirits conspire around me eager to help.
It is time to create what my heart and soul once dreamed of.
My mind chimes in, "You cannot do this!"
Oh, but my heart and soul know differently.
"You can create anything.
Just allow!" my soul whispers.
"Can I quiet my mind or maybe weave my mind
and soul together to work as a team?"
Just allow!

I let go ... and pour a rainbow of colors on my palette.
I ask for help.
My intuitive voice speaks to me in faint
yet powerful voices giving me clues.
I pick up my brush and allow something spectacular
to move through me.
A love affair has begun with this blank vastness of white,
I feel as close to God as one can get . . .
Allowing, collaborating, creating, playing, loving, being
but mostly surrendering.
My brush has descended deep into my soul,
and I have created a story on something
that was once a blank canvas.

Art Heals

"Art is a safe place where you can freely express

all of your emotions and heal."

- Christine Burke

To work with Christine one on one, to schedule a paint party or workshop or to hire Christine for a speaking event email info@liveyourcreativtiy.com.

To view her art prints and accessories go to – http://www.liveyourcreativity.com/prints/ or http://bit.ly/christineburkeart.

To purchase original art work by Christine visit http://www.liveyourcreativity.com/original-paintings/ to view and email info@liveyourcreativity.com to inquire.

Benefits of adding creativity to your life

- It can help you concentrate and focus.
- Keeps you in the present moment and helps with managing worry and stress.
- It can boost your self-confidence and provides a sense of gratification, accomplishment and a sense of purpose.
- Helps if you feel blocked in any areas of your life.
- It relaxes you.
- It can help you understand your emotions, and it is a safe place to express all of your feelings.
- It can boost your immune system and reduce inflammation. Recently, scientists are finding that art heals. These findings suggest that merely looking at creative works, enjoying nature or listening to music can boost your immune system and reduce inflammation. So, imagine what creating one of these works can do for you.

"When the artist is alive within us, we become stimulating, creative beings from whom everyone around us can benefit."

- Bernie Siegel

Benefits of nourishing your body and inner artist

- Improves your mood.
- Boost your energy.
- Give you clarity so you can focus on your creative work.
- Reduces inflammation in your body, which can help prevent disease.

"I believe the greatest gift you can give your family and the world is a healthy you."

- Joyce Meyer

This book was inspired by my experience at the Institute for Integrative Nutrition® (IIN), where I received my training in holistic wellness and health coaching.

IIN offers a truly comprehensive Health Coach Training Program that invites students to deeply explore the things that are most nourishing to them. From the physical aspects of nutrition and eating wholesome foods that work best for each individual person, to the concept of Primary Food – the idea that everything in life, including our spirituality, career, relationships, and fitness contributes to our inner and outer health – IIN helped me reach optimal health and balance. This inner journey unleashed the passion that compels me to share what I've learned and inspire others.

Beyond personal health, IIN offers training in health coaching, as well as business and marketing. Students who choose to pursue this field professionally complete the program equipped with the communication skills and branding knowledge they need to create a fulfilling career encouraging and supporting others in reaching their own health goals.

From renowned wellness experts as Visiting Teachers to the convenience of their online learning platform, this school has changed my life, and I believe it will do the same for you. I invite you to learn more about the Institute for Integrative Nutrition and explore how the Health Coach Training Program can help you transform your life. Feel free to contact me to hear more about my personal experience at http://www.liveyourcreativity.com/iin-ambassador/ or call (844) 315-8546 to learn more.

ACKNOWLEDGMENTS

It takes a village to do anything in this world and it sure took one to write this book. I am grateful for the following fellow travelers in life who helped me create this book.

To My Children

Angela and Thomas, my two favorite creations. I am so glad you chose me to be your mother. I am so grateful I chose art over alcohol; it enables me to mother you instead of smother you.

To My First Family

My mom, dad, Cathy, Jimmy and Gina — I love our memories and our unconditional love. Thanks for supporting, accepting and helping my art spirit grow.

To all my aunts, uncles, cousins and relatives who completed my family. A special shout out to the fellow art spirits in the family — Aunt Cassy, Uncle Eddie, Eileen and my mom.

To My Friends and Fellow Travelers in this Life

To all my childhood friends — our memories, camaraderie and fun times take up a special place in my heart. Especially to my childhood friend Beth who has been by my side for almost 40 years. My sidekick, my soul friend and the co-creator of Inspired Action Meditation.

A special thank you to my college friend, although we don't see each other as much anymore, our connection runs deep.

To John C, I am grateful that serendipity brought you into my life. Your cooking expertise helped my right brain focus and establish all the measurement for my recipes that were in my head. I am also grateful for your love and support.

To Karl, a kindred art spirit, who taught me everything I ever needed to know about painting (and life).

To Melanie Ericksen, healer and dear friend, I am grateful that you are on this journey with me.

To the friends I met at every stage of life, each and every one of you has helped me grow and to the friends who I have yet to meet on this journey.

To My Clients and all Who Attend My Workshops and Paint Parties

You are all an inspiration to me and help me keep going. I continue to learn from you every day. Thanks to all of you who allowed me to share your stories in this book. A special thank you to Kathy Samworth and Rich Shane. These stories connect us all. I hope this book connects you even deeper to your art spirit and nourishes your mind, body and soul.

To Lisa Fugard

An amazing editor, thank you for helping me dig deeper into the book and my life.

To Amie Olson

A fabulous book designer, thank you for designing the cover and interior of this book.

To Joshua Rosenthal, founder of the Institute for Integrative Nutrition®

I am forever grateful for this program that helps me to continue to learn and grow.

To the lady at the lunch place who led me to The Institute for Integrative Nutrition.

Love and Gratitude!

Christine ❤

RESOURCES

Henri, Robert. *The Art Spirit*. Philadelphia: Lippincott, 1923. Print.

Cameron, Julia. *The Artist's Way*. New York: G.P. Putnam's Sons, 1992. Print.

Seiferle, Rebecca. "Romanticism Movement Overview and Analysis." TheArt-Story.org. 2018. Web. <http://www.theartstory.org/movement-romanticism.htm>

Sarah, Ban Breathnach, Sarah. *Simple Abundance*. New York: Warner Books, Inc, 1995.

Ford, Debbie. *The Dark Side of The Light Chasers*. California: Hay House, Inc, 1998.

Brown, Brené. *Braving the Wilderness*. New York: Random House, 2017.

Kelce, Jason. Super Bowl parade speech: Full Transcript. The Inquirer. Web. 08 Feb. 2018<http://www.philly.com/philly/super-bowl-lii/jason-kelce-eagles-parade-speech-philadelphia-super-bowl-full-text-20180208.html>.

Thomsen, Robert. *Bill W*. New York: Harper & Row Publishers, Inc, 1975. Print.

Silver, Tosha. *Outrageous Openness: Letting the Divine Take the Lead*. New York: Simon & Schuster, Inc, 2014. Print.

Baron-Reid, Colette. *Wisdom of the Oracle*. California: Hay House, Inc, 2015. Print.

Virtue, Doreen. *Saints & Angels Oracle Cards*. California: Hay House, Inc, 2005. Print.

Roth, Geneen. *Breaking Free from Emotional Eating*. New York: Plume, A Member of Penguin Group, Inc, 2004. Print.

"EWG's 2018 Shopper's Guide to Pesticides in Produce." EWG. 2017. Website.

<https://www.ewg.org/foodnews/>

"Art Does Heal: Scientists Say Appreciating Creative Works Can Fight Off Disease." The Telegraph. 10 Feb. 2015. Web. <https://www.telegraph.co.uk/news/health/news/11403404/Art-does-heal-scientists-say-appreciating-creative-works-can-fight-off-disease.html>